The Disadvantages of Inequality

Richard Berthoud

The Disadvantages
of Inequality

A Study of Social Deprivation

A PEP REPORT
MACDONALD AND JANE'S · LONDON

Copyright © PEP 1976

First published in Great Britain in 1976 by
Macdonald and Jane's Publishers Limited
Paulton House
8 Shepherdess Walk
London N1 7LW

ISBN: 0 354 04047 2

Printed in Great Britain by
REDWOOD BURN LIMITED
Trowbridge & Esher

Contents

Preface

This book is the report on a review of fact and opinion on the subject of 'multiple deprivation' carried out by the author at PEP. The research was kindly sponsored by a grant from the Gatsby Charitable Foundation. A small 'depth interview' survey among deprived families was carried out for PEP by the Centre for Sample Surveys.

PEP is most grateful to all those who assisted in the research by providing material, by discussing their own work, or by commenting on drafts of the report. Particular acknowledgement should be made of the help of the experts in various fields who formed an advisory committee under the chairmanship of Dr Mark Abrams.

Introduction

Throughout the nineteenth century and the first half of the twentieth, the new middle-class conscience and working-class consciousness worked to obtain for 'the people' those reasonable conditions of life that were seen as the unfair privileges of an elite minority. They were concerned that the 'masses' should have reasonable housing, reasonable sanitation, reasonable conditions of work, reasonable wages, reasonable education, reasonable medical services and so on. Many would claim that those aims are a fair way towards achievement, even if others would assert that for every improvement in working-class prosperity there has been an equivalent improvement for the middle classes, thus maintaining the original gap unchanged. Certainly the 1950s, and the dawn of the so-called 'Affluent Society', showed a marked decline in concern for the underprivileged, on the assumption that a booming economy and the welfare state had solved the problems of the 'people as a whole'. Isolated cases of indigence were not held to destroy this conclusion – they could be explained in terms of personal characteristics, about which little could be done beyond the provision of psychiatrically orientated social work.

During the 1960s, however, social research was revealing a number of ways in which provisions for 'the people as a whole' were failing to secure satisfactory standards for *everybody*, and that these failures, in spite of afflicting only a minority, were too frequent and too systematic to be brushed aside as isolated cases. Social concern for the underprivileged was therefore revived, after a relatively short lull; only the concern was now felt for the *minority* in relation to the rest of society. Thus the bird's-eye view of the masses has given way to a worm's-eye view, as we seek policies to raise the conditions of life for the few up to the standards expected by the people as a whole. The talk is no longer so much about privileges as about deprivation. Since society has probably always contained an unlucky minority, as well as

9

a moderate majority and a lucky minority, this concern about deprivation may constitute more of a change in the way we look at society than in the structure of society itself.

Policies are, of course, directed with varying degrees of success at the various particular problems which have been shown to persist: low incomes, unemployment, poor housing and so on. But it has also become apparent that certain types of people are especially likely to suffer these problems, whichever particular policy field is under consideration: these are the elderly, immigrants, large families, one-parent families, residents of particular inner city areas, the physically or mentally handicapped, and so on. This fact has called attention to the probability that the different kinds of deprivation go together, and that some people, and some families, suffer many different problems at once. They have become known as *multiply-deprived.*

Quite a lot is now known about each of the particular social misfortunes that can be grouped under the label of deprivation. Quite a lot is known, and more is being found out, about the combined incidence of these misfortunes in particular groups in the population, whether such groups are identified by their demographic characteristics (old people, children, immigrants) or by their geographical location (inner city areas). But, in spite of the acceptance of the term 'multiple deprivation' into the jargon of social commentary, very little is known about multiplicity itself, taking into account all the social problems and all the types of people there are. Since neither the multiply-deprived, nor multiple deprivation, has been defined empirically, it is not possible to take measurements that would exactly identify who suffers, and who escapes. There is, however, a good deal of indirect evidence with which to approach such questions. The purpose of this book is to collate some of the facts and opinions that are available in the field and to consider the incidence of various social misfortunes in different groups in the population, in order to reach some tentative conclusions about the nature of multiple deprivation as a general problem, in relation to those aspects of inequality that are considered to be acceptable.

There are strong *a priori* grounds for supposing that social misfortunes afflict people or families three or four at a time. After all, poor people do not often live in mansions, nor do rich people live in slums. If it is poor people who live in slums, then at least two deprivations (of income and of housing) go together in pairs. The most obvious explanation for multiple deprivation thus lies in a cycle of mutual causation, based on a simple market model. Starting, say, with a man's lack of job skills, we would expect him to be limited to a poorly paid job, or even unemployment. The consequent low income limits his family's choice in the housing market to a decrepit house, probably in an environmentally unsatisfactory area. Further disadvantages may stem from the bad housing and the poor environment, and so on. Thus a cycle of mutual causation and reinforcement, with, perhaps, income as the central controlling factor, can be put forward to help predict or explain multiple deprivation.

It is not, however, possible to rely entirely on a theory set out in terms of scientific causes leading to inevitable effects to explain the incidence and coincidence of the deprivations that are the subject of this book. The incidence of some aspects of deprivation–of education and of health, for instance–cannot be ascribed simply to the distribution of income according to a market model. Secondly, it is difficult to explain why one family, in a certain time and place, should suffer misfortunes that are avoided by an apparently identical family in another time and place. Thirdly, although in general it is the poorer households that have, say, poorer quality housing, it is by no means always the poorest households that suffer the worst housing. The closer the examination of the particular incidence of social misfortunes, the more it appears that we are looking at *accidents*–not just accidents in the conventional sense of accidental injury, but also in the wider sense of a particular coincidence of circumstances affecting an individual for better or worse. If a man happens to work in a factory that closes down, if he happens to live in an area where there is an acute housing shortage, if he happens to fall ill, if he happens to have had a particularly unsympathetic schoolteacher–if any of these things happen, then deprivation may be a consequence. The direct interaction of misfortunes may then make his situation even worse. Alternatively, a run of good luck could raise him to an unexpected level of prosperity.

It should not, of course, be inferred from the use of the term accident that these things strike at random throughout society. As will be seen again and again in this book, the accidents are almost monopolised by the manual working class, and concentrated in the unskilled lower working class. To continue to use the vocabulary of the metaphor, it could be said that these classes are accident-prone. If one group of people is highly likely to suffer any of a range of kinds of social accident, then different misfortunes can be expected to be associated, and some people to be multiply-deprived, even before any account is taken of the probable tendency of one problem to lead directly to another.

We need to know more about the complex web of association between the different aspects of deprivation in order to understand any direct interactions, and to discover exactly which groups in the population are most at risk. But, if the concept of the social accident is a useful way of looking at these problems, then it will also be valuable to look at the origins of each kind of misfortune separately, in an attempt to find out why it is that the same people are so vulnerable to each of them. That is the purpose of this book, making use of such information as is already available. It should lead towards some tentative conclusions on the twin aims of future policy: to reduce the number of social accidents which occur at all, and to reduce the propensity of certain types of people to be the ones who suffer.

The terms 'deprivation' and 'multiple deprivation' conjure up different ideas for different people. For some, it is a problem of cultural deprivation experienced by the children of a certain kind of parent. For others, it means certain deviant anti-social forms of behaviour. For the purpose of this book, however, we maintain the distinction expressed by the juvenile delinquent in *West Side Story*, who claimed he was 'depraved on account of I'm deprived'. In the book deprivations are considered to be mainly socio-economic situational problems, in which the citizen lacks something most other people have – money, housing, health, a good job and so on. Behavioural problems may or may not be a cause or an effect of deprivation, but they do not in themselves constitute a deprivation within our definition.

Because of this definition of deprivation as a lack of something other people have, the first chapter of this book discusses the general concepts of *inequality and poverty* – using income as its main focus – in order to decide how to judge whether one person's situation is sufficiently below that of other people's to constitute deprivation. There is also a discussion of the concepts of fairness and unfairness. The second chapter looks at some aspects of our *Social Security* provisions, in particular the value of the work incentive, and the very wide range of different benefits all seeking to achieve the same result. In the third chapter the slow improvement in the size and quality of our *housing* stock is contrasted with the rapid rise in homelessness in recent years. The subject of the fourth chapter is *children,* and the relation between inequality, education and the theory of socialisation is discussed. The fifth chapter presents some old and some new evidence on the differences between manual and non-manual workers in *employment.* The sixth chapter examines the widely discussed but little understood *geographical variations* in deprivation, especially the problem of the inner city.

The subject matter of each of these first six chapters already commands an extensive literature of its own. It is not, of course, possible in a single book to do full justice to each subject, and an expert in any one of the fields may feel that some emphases have been misplaced in the treatment. But it is necessary, from time to time, for research about various particular policy issues to be examined from a single point of view, in order to reach more general conclusions. In the final chapter much of the evidence from preceding chapters is used to provide the basis for a more general discussion of the relation between inequality and deprivation. All sorts of social misfortune are found to be concentrated on particular 'socially weak' groups in society. It is not possible to explain deprivation either *solely* in terms of the personal characteristics of the individual, or *solely* in terms of the circumstances in which the individual finds himself. But a determined policy to improve the opportunities of disadvantaged groups should result in a narrowing of the gap between prosperity and deprivation, without undermining the operation of a free economy.

Two general notes

1. Most of the facts on which this book is based are derived from various statistics furnished on a regular basis by government departments. Unfortunately the important statistical series vary considerably, both in the gap between enquiries and in the speed with which results are published. This means that it is impossible to quote all statistics for the same year.

The only way of basing all statistics on the same year would be to look back at 1971. In general such consistency has been rejected in favour of quoting the most recent sources. The disadvantage of this approach is particularly acute with monetary statistics: for instance, in Chapter 2 it is necessary to refer to the 1976 scale of Supplementary Benefit rates, 1975 wage rates (from the *New Earnings Survey*) and 1974 data about the distribution of benefits (from *Social Security Statistics*). Supplementary Benefit rates increased 52 per cent between mid-1974 and mid-1976 for ordinary claimants, and 68 per cent for long-term claimants.

At the time of going to press (Summer, 1976) the latest editions of the most important series are as follows:

Census of Population	1971
General Household Survey	1973
Family Expenditure Survey	1974
Social Security Statistics	1974
Social Trends	1974
New Earnings Survey	1975
Housing and Construction Statistics	1975

2. One of the most important analyses throughout this book is based on occupational status. Workers (and their families) are divided between manual and non-manual occupations (see Table 1). Within manual, the subdivision is usually between skilled, semi-skilled and unskilled; and within the non-manual group, between managerial and professional on the one hand, and intermediate and junior non-manual on the other. Unfortunately, because no ideal definition of occupational status exists, there is some variety between sources in the definitions of the different groups, and variety too in the terminology – 'social class', 'social grade', 'socio-economic group', 'occupational status', and so on. Since this book is based on a variety of sources, it has not been possible to use one definition consistently. But, just as none of the definitions is ideal, so all of them divide the population pretty consistently, and it is necessary to assume that where large differences occur between groups, such differences are not very sensitive to the precise definition. It is, for instance, possible to show that there is not much difference between the classifications 'social class' and 'socio-economic group'. If analysis is based on five general groups, 89 per cent of heads of household fall into the same category whichever definition is applied (see Table 1). The only serious inconsistency is that 'ancillary workers and artists' are allocated to 'social class I/II' but are not in the top 'socio-economic group' category.

Table 1 Heads of household cross-divided by social class and socio-economic group (global percentages)

	Social Class					
	Professional/ intermediate	Other non-manual	Skilled manual	Semi-skilled manual	Unskilled manual	Not classified
Socio-economic group	I/II	IIIn	IIIm	IV	V	
Managers, professionals (1-4, 13)	15	∅	—	∅	—	—
Other non-manual (5, 6)	5	12	—	2	—	—
Skilled manual (8, 9, 12, 14)	2	∅	29	1	∅	—
Semi-skilled manual (7, 10, 15)	—	∅	1	14	—	—
Unskilled manual (11)	—	—	—	—	6	—
Not classified (16, 17)	—	—	—	—	—	13

∅=more than zero, less than 0.5%
From the 1971 census, derived from Table 39 of *Social Trends, No 5, 1974*. Socio-economic groups have been collapsed to five groups as in the General Household Survey

1 Inequality

Very often the problems that are considered under the heading of 'deprivation' arise when a person's or a family's situation is distinctly different from normal: no job, when most men have jobs; physical disability, when most people are fit; no bathroom, when most houses have one; and so on. In such cases it may seem easy to define deprivation in various fields. On the other hand, there are some aspects of life where a clean division between the satisfactory and the inadequate is not possible. At what point does income become 'too low', or hours of work 'excessive', for example? Moreover, before deprivation in particular fields can be discussed, it is necessary to understand how any set of circumstances is said to constitute inadequacy. Why is lack of a bathroom considered intolerable when not so long ago running hot water would have been considered the limit of necessary plumbing, and even that an innovation? Why is the label 'poor' given to families whose purchasing power is princely in comparison with hundreds of millions in Africa and Asia?

Before it is possible to discuss different kinds of deprivation, therefore, it is necessary to consider ideas about inequality and fairness. Monetary income is used as the central focus for this discussion, but many of the conclusions can be applied just as well to other factors.

Understanding poverty

Analysis of the distribution of incomes can be undertaken with reference to three different concepts: *the standard of living, inequality* and *poverty*. Much of the argument that takes place is about the relative importance of these three concepts rather than disagreement about any one of them, and it is therefore helpful to try to distinguish clearly between them.

A LOW STANDARD OF LIVING is concerned with the quantity of goods and services that can be bought by people with their income. Although the reference point is theoretically a 'basket' of goods and services, the concept is generally used to compare a society, or a section of society, either with itself at a past or future period or with some other society.

INEQUALITY is concerned with some people having less than others, the others being either the average or the comparatively rich. The reference point is other members of the same society.

POVERTY is concerned with people who have not *enough* to live on decently. How we decide how much is 'enough' will be discussed later; the point now is that the concept of poverty means people having less than some minimum income. This is not the only possible meaning of the word poverty, but it is the meaning implied in its use by social scientists.

There is not much doubt that the *standard of living* of this country has risen immensely, if not continuously, nor in line with that in some other western developed countries, during this century. If the standard of living were the only criterion, then it would be indisputable that we have 'never had it so good'. Almost all sections of society can now buy more goods and services than they could, for instance, before the First World War. An entirely accurate comparison is not possible, both because the early data on earnings are probably not very reliable, and also because comparison of the purchasing power of the pound over a long period is of uncertain value. Nevertheless, if we allow for the pound to be worth one-twelfth of its pre-1914 value[1], the statistics give a pretty clear conclusion (Table 2).

Table 2   Weekly earnings of male manual workers, 1906 and 1975[2]

	Lowest decile*	Lower quartile*	Median*	Upper quartile*	Highest decile*
1906 earnings	£ 1.0	£ 1.2	£ 1.5	£ 1.9	£ 2.3
1906 at 1975 prices	£12.0	£14.4	£18.0	£22.8	£27.6
1975 earnings	£36.8	£44.1	£53.2	£64.5	£76.9

* If a representative group of 100 workers is placed in order of earnings, the lowest decile gives the earnings of the tenth from the bottom, the lower quartile the twenty-fifth from the bottom, the median the fiftieth, the upper quartile the seventy-fifth, and the highest decile the ninetieth.

As far as manual workers are concerned, all groups have increased their real purchasing power about threefold. This applies as much to the lowest paid as to the average; the 1975 manual worker who was tenth from the bottom earned considerably more, in real terms, than the 1906 worker who was tenth from the top.

Moreover, even if a family man with three children was out of work in 1975, and receiving Supplementary Benefit, he would have getting on for £35 per week, assuming he paid average rent and rates. That would give him a purchasing power equivalent to a highly paid manual worker in 1906. Similarly, the standard of living of most people, perhaps even of all people, living in Britain today, is, if measured simply in terms of purchasing power, far higher than that of most people living in many countries in Africa and Asia, even if it is lower than in Sweden or America.

So, if we used a wide historical or geographical perspective, there might be grounds for rejoicing in our average standard of living, and even satisfaction with the purchasing power of the poorest members of society. The important question concerns the choice of perspective. If each person, or each family, was concerned solely with his or her own survival in the face of natural dangers of starvation or exposure, then most of the poorest people in Britain today could get by. If they were able to live by reference to the millions of people in other ages, or other continents, who were or are unable to count on survival, they might congratulate themselves. Unfortunately people's lives are primarily contrasted with their immediate neighbours in time and space. Since social standards are set by our own society, the income of the man who earned £35 a week in 1975 must be compared with his neighbour's £45, the man at the end of the street's £55, and the man in the next street's £65. It is universally accepted that the apparent *monetary* value of incomes has to be adjusted for the changing value of money to reach their *real* value; it is less widely realised how the apparent real value has to be adjusted for changing values in society to assess their *social* value.

There are many reasons why incomes have to be evaluated in terms of social norms. Envy, or keeping up with the Joneses, is by no means the whole of the story, although it is part of it. Nor can envy be disparaged in the poor, if the pattern of inequality is supposed to be justified by its role of stimulating the poor to better themselves.

But the problem is deeper than that. Life as it is lived is a highly social activity; that is the reason why mental subnormalities or illnesses that entirely desocialise a person make him incapable of 'living' as we understand the word. Money is itself a social institution.

The social norm therefore defines the social standard, and those who fall below such a standard must be considered socially deprived. Just as there are some things – radios, sports, buses, and so on – which would be rendered not only unnecessary but impossible if other people were irrelevant, so there are other things – clothes, hot baths, cups of tea and so on – which have been specified as necessities by current society.

Few will be found to deny that the wearing of clothes in public on a hot summer's day is not physically necessary to survival, but is nevertheless socially necessary, and that inability to afford clothes constitutes deprivation, even in summer. In order to decide whether the incomes of the poorest members of society are adequate or not, however, one is tempted to distinguish necessities from luxuries, either on the basis of value judgements of each item or by dividing commodities into strata: primary physical necessities, secondary social necessities, tertiary social desirables, quaternary social luxuries, and so on.

The first method, of value judgements, may lead one to decide that, say, television is an entirely unnecessary item – even some wealthy people do not bother with one – and as such is a luxury. Since even the poorest members of society are likely to have a television set,[3] the conclusion is often reached that current low incomes are satisfactory, perhaps excessive. Unfortunately the distinction between a necessity and a luxury is not easily made by those who can afford both. An objective definition of a social necessity is an item people are least prepared to sacrifice, leaving for luxuries those items people can (in practice) do without; and the measurements must be done by the section of society that actually has to make the choice. On this basis television has become a necessity, fresh fruit a luxury. (If you object to claiming television as a necessity, how about electric light, hot baths and children's Christmas presents? None of them is strictly necessary, but all are extremely difficult to sacrifice.)

The alternative approach may be to categorise commodities according to the importance of the basic purposes they serve. Physical survival being of overriding importance, items contributing to physical health will be considered to be first-order necessities. If there is enough money in the household budget for a decent diet, then a first stage of adequacy has been achieved. This approach also breaks down, in a similar way to the first, when we find that mothers who *could* afford to feed themselves reasonably nevertheless live on toast in order to buy Christmas presents for their children. If physical necessity takes second place to social necessity, then an income that was *de jure* sufficient for a proper diet is seen to be *de facto* inadequate.

The point has perhaps been most graphically illustrated by Professor Townsend, in simply quoting the minimum standards laid down in 1899. 'Who would dare,' asks Townsend, 'to lay down a scale of necessities for the 1970s for young women in Britain consisting of:

One pair of boots
Two aprons
One second-hand dress
One skirt made from an old dress
A third of the cost of a new hat
A third of the cost of a shawl and a jacket
Two pairs of stockings
A few unspecified underclothes
One pair of stays
and One pair of old boots worn as slippers.'[4]

Who would dare? Who, indeed, would even want to, however brave?

A given 'objective' standard of living has therefore to be evaluated in terms of what is usual in the society in which the subject is living, for social sanctions towards conformity seem to be often as powerful as the physical sanctions of hunger and cold. Of course, the social sanction is rarely as absolute and overt as that employed in the earlier example of the wearing of clothes in public places in summer. The sanctions may vary in their nature and in their power in different times, places and classes, and for different aspects of life. There is, however, a more general social sanction, which inhibits people from taking a 'sensible' independent attitude to their spending priorities. This is based on the persistent view that a man's money is a direct measure of his worth in society. As long as those with more money feel intrinsically superior to those with less money, the latter will feel intrinsically inferior not only in public but also within their own homes. And as the distribution of income is more and more defended in meritocratic terms, the more powerful such sanctions become. It is because of this that it may be so much easier for the obviously well off to take such 'sensible' decisions as buying second-hand clothes or forgoing television sets than for the less well off, for whom such behaviour would involve exposure.

Many of these points will recur later in this chapter, and in later chapters. The conclusion is that incomes of the lowest paid must be measured in comparison with the rest of society, not in comparison with other ages or other nations. Perhaps the case for concern about inequality in society has been most simply expressed by pointing out that today, as in the past, some people can exchange the product of their labour for little more than half the product of the average man's labour, whereas others can buy the product of five men's labour.

Turning back to Table 2 on p. 18, we can calculate that in 1906 the 'lowest decile' manual worker's earnings were 67 per cent of the 'median' and 43 per cent of the 'highest decile'. In 1974 the 'lowest decile' was 69 per cent of the 'median' and 48 per cent of the 'highest decile'. The earnings of the lowest paid can therefore scarcely be considered to be much improved over this long period of time.

After the Second World War two major changes took place in Britain. Firstly, full (or almost full) employment became normal, putting an end to the massive dole queues of the inter-war period. Secondly, the Labour Party gained real power for the first time, and started to put into operation a range of policies designed directly to combat inequality, policies far wider than the already considerable programme of the Liberals before the First World War. Some, like the National Health Service, provided free treatment for all, thereby either increasing the benefit or decreasing the cost of benefits to the poorest. Others, like National Insurance and National Assistance, gave a state income to people who otherwise would have received little or no income.

Working from theory, these changes, combined with progressive taxation on income, could have been expected to reduce inequality in society, not only among manual workers but across the whole range from the richest to the poorest. That was the intention, and that, for many years, was widely agreed to be the result. This consensus 'found expression in a steady stream – at times almost a torrent – of books, pamphlets, articles and newspaper editorials . . . condemning the egalitarian effects of full employment, the reduction of differences in earnings and rewards for work, high progressive taxation and the "Welfare State".'

So said Professor Titmuss[5] in 1962. In criticising previous analyses of income, and concluding that income, if properly measured, showed a very similar pattern of inequality to that before 1939, he, in turn, launched 'a steady stream – at times almost a torrent' of authoritative works demonstrating a consistent, perhaps even an increasing, pattern of inequality. That stream has continued through to the 1970s, but now it seems that both streams are flowing side by side. On the 'left' there are those who continue to argue that inequality is as bad as ever, if not getting worse, and on the 'right' there are those, like Sir Keith Joseph, the Institute of Economic Affairs, and the 'Black Paper' group of educationalists, who are again arguing that weakening inequality is undermining the work incentive. Neither side appears to believe that whatever is happening is a 'good thing'; both 'left' and 'right' are in agreement that something is wrong.

It is almost impossible to obtain all the information necessary to deduce the extent of inequality in society even for one year, much less for a series of years so that trends could be analysed. Even if the information was to hand, interpretation would not be easy.[6] The calculations that seem to have been based on the widest data on incomes, taxes and benefits appear to show that, although the distribution of taxes and benefits makes society less unequal than it would have been if everyone kept and depended on their original incomes, the net degree of inequality has not changed at a time when it would be expected to change (Table 3).

Table 3   Measures of overall inequality, 1961-1971[7]
('Gini coefficient'*)

	1961-2	1971
Original income	31.3	34.0
Income after all taxes and benefits	24.3	25.0

*The Gini coefficient is one of many statistics intended to show the extent to which incomes are unequal. If all households had the same income, the coefficient would be 0; if one household had all the income, it would be 100.

Similar (admittedly approximate) calculations of the same measure as in Table 3 for the year 1937 gave figures of 33 before taxes and 25 after – virtually identical to the figures for a quarter of a century later.

Although it may be possible to suggest that income gaps for particular sections of society may be widening or narrowing, there is really no firm evidence of a general shift one way or another. Without that evidence we may have to conclude that relative distribution remains pretty well constant, as the total prosperity of the nation improves.

From the point of view of the poorest households, under pressure from the social norm, it could be suggested that we are running fast only to stand still. This is too dismal a conclusion. If we use the apparent consistency in the degree of inequality to argue that 'the poor' are just as poor as they ever were, we would also have to conclude that the average family is no better off, and the rich are no richer. This is wholly to deny any benefit at all from generally increasing prosperity. Such a position is not, of course, untenable, but it is difficult to square with the view that poverty is a social evil, since that view contains a considerable materialist element. Perhaps a more reasonable view would be that, although a reduction in inequality may be preferable to an increase in prosperity, the latter is better than nothing. But the figures do refute the belief that greater prosperity automatically leads to greater equality; it may perhaps be a necessary condition, but it turns out not to be a sufficient condition.

It is, in fact, possible to return to the theory of income deprivation relative to the social norm, to show why it is not possible to analyse inequality entirely independently of changing prosperity when measuring 'poverty'. A measure of inequality is specific to a given place at a given point in time. Society, and social values, are not entirely confined in time and place, however. If a nation is highly prosperous in comparison with its history, or with other parts of the world, then the social norm against which a family's income will be compared will take some account of the extent of indigence known to exist in other times or other places – not much perhaps, but some. But a probably more important effect will derive from the shorter term dynamics of the local society. In a period of rapidly changing prosperity the social norm that is postulated as the bench-mark against which individual incomes are measured will always lag some way behind the level it would reach in a static situation. This is because people live through the dynamic period, and their values will be affected by their memories, as well as by their current experience. Memories of the slump are relevant; so are memories of our generally lower standard of living five or ten years ago.

On this argument, perhaps the best way of assessing the income status of a family would be to compare current income with the national average of five years earlier (correcting for changing prices). Unfortunately there is no empirical way of deciding whether the bench-mark should be placed five years or two years or ten years earlier. But if an index of this sort were to be used, then, if the degree of inequality remained constant:

1 In a period of generally increasing prosperity a comparatively small proportion of people would feel poor (compared with a static situation).
2 In a period of generally declining prosperity a comparatively large proportion of people would feel poor.
3 When a period of increasing prosperity gives way to a period of static prosperity, the proportion of people who feel poor must go up.

This last is a conclusion of the first consequence in the context of the halt of real economic growth that took place in 1974. The concern often shown that the poorest should obtain what little extra becomes available during this period is not a gesture for improvement but is necessary to prevent the situation getting worse.[8]

After the *standard of living* and *inequality* the third important concept mentioned at the beginning of this chapter was *poverty*. The word has already been used in a loose way in the preceding discussion. Indeed the modern concept of poverty has been described – we think of people as 'poor' if their incomes are insufficient for a proper life, both 'sufficiency' and 'a proper life' being derived socially. It then seems desirable to define a 'poverty line' in order to count 'the poor'.

In 1899 Seebohm Rowntree counted the number of poor families in York.[9] His 'poverty line' was derived by deciding what commodities a family needed to buy in order to subsist. A family without sufficient income to buy these commodities was considered 'poor'. A similar York survey in 1936 showed the extent of poverty to have increased,[10] but in 1951 it seemed to have virtually disappeared,[11] using the Rowntree definition.

This reinforced the general complacency about poverty in the 1950s, which has already been referred to. But in the 1960s Professors Abel-Smith and Townsend argued that 'the poor' should be defined as those living at or about the minimum standard of living officially tolerated by the State.[12] They showed not only that 18 per cent were on this poverty line in 1960, but also that 10 per cent should have been so defined even in the early 1950s – a direct contradiction of Rowntree's more optimistic conclusion.

Rowntree's commodity-based and theoretically fixed subsistence level was apparently a standard-of-living measure, and was subject to the criticisms of inflexibility to social change that have been dealt with earlier in this chapter. The 'rediscovery of poverty' of the 1960s was based on the Abel-Smith/Townsend use of the National Assistance rates, which were offered as the nearest measure to our 'social norm' that could be found.[13] Actually, the difference between the two definitions was far more theoretical than real:

1 Rowntree's subsistence budget made allowance for social conventional items, which were not necessary for survival, e.g. tea.
2 Rowntree changed his commodity list from survey to survey, and was therefore partly conventional, not inflexible.
3 The National Assistance scales on which the Abel-Smith/Townsend definition was based were themselves based on Rowntree-like subsistence calculations.
4 The two definitions, however derived, were very similar in practice. York may have been exceptionally prosperous, for when the Rowntree definition is applied to the Abel-Smith/Townsend national data, the results are not dissimilar:

Table 4   Distribution of household standards of living,[14]

	1953-4	
	Rowntree subsistence level= 100	*National Assistance scale= 100*
(per cent)	*(per cent)*	*(per cent)*
Below 100	5.4	2.1
100-19	4.5	3.6
120-39	6.0	4.4
140 or more	84.1	89.9

The Rowntree subsistence level seems to have been equivalent to 120 per cent of the N.A. scale.

Both methods therefore produce similar results. The subsistence-scale method (which was also applied in the United States in the 1960s, subject to the same criticisms, and also much more conventional than its authors admit[15]) has the disadvantage that it requires up-dating to account for changing conventions each time it is used, but there is no objective basis for carrying out the up-dating.[16] The state-minimum method is more sensitive to changing conventions, but is also unfortunately the joint expression of two social conventions –it reflects society's view not only of what income constitutes poverty, but also of what the state should do about it. If the state decides to be more generous in its fight against poverty, the number of poor people will appear to increase.[17] As it happens, the British government has kept the ratio of guaranteed income to average earnings fairly constant since the Second World War,[18] so that the method makes a useful measure of inequality; but it need not continue to do so.

The debate about how to define the poverty line now seems to have died down. The attempts at counting the number of 'poor' people during the 1960s were vital in drawing public attention to the continuing problems of living on a low income. Analytically they were less useful. The implication of saying 'There are x million poor' must be that 'There should be none at all, and that progress towards that goal should be measured'. The goal of total elimination is, however, at issue with the concept of relativity on which present-day analysis is based. For centuries poverty meant starvation or near-starvation; it meant the risk of death through exposure to the elements; it meant eating one meal without knowing where tomorrow's or next week's meals were coming from; it meant sudden increases in mortality during seasons of agricultural failure; it allowed for Malthusian doctrines on natural forces in population limitation; it led to begging or stealing through economic necessity. In these senses it had some truly absolute meaning; its elimination was a useful goal, which has been largely achieved in Britain today, if not elsewhere in the world.[19]

We are still worried about poverty but we have redefined a new kind of poverty, not rediscovered the old. Relative poverty is, unlike the absolute poverty described above, by definition ineradicable. The 'social norm' will always be above the level of those who are right at the bottom of the distribution of income. The poor, as people are fond of reminding us, will always be with us. The focus is therefore no longer on counting how many people are below some poverty line, but analysing who is living at the bottom of the ladder, in order to assess how best to narrow the gap between them and the rest of society. Perhaps poverty is not so much a condition that individuals suffer but an abstract; it is that part of inequality which is excessive, unnecessary and unfair.

Many of these arguments meet in the theory of 'Relative Deprivation', which was given its main empirical base in 1966 by W. G. Runciman.[20] The theory is that people tend to form *reference groups,* against which to measure their own situation. They will feel relatively deprived if they do not have what their reference groups have. In other words, people compare themselves with other people, and feel relatively deprived if they come badly out of the comparison. A reference group might be a specific group of people (members of the person's own class, or neighbourhood, or some other class or neighbourhood); it might be less immediate (the sort of person one used to be); or it might even be hypothetical (the sort of person one had hoped to be). The theory is obviously closely connected with our earlier discussion of the 'social norm'.

One reason why a generally increasing standard of living is desirable, even if inequality remains constant, is that among a person's reference groups will be himself-five-years-ago and his-neighbour-five-years-ago. Increasing prosperity means that deprivation is reduced relative to his historical reference group, even though the person is just as deprived relative to his neighbour's current situation.

In theory one could make a reference group of any person, or group of people, whatever their position in society. We can all aspire to either being, or meeting, Robert Redford, depending on our sex. On looking at the theory more closely, however, it seems more likely that one will compare oneself with reference groups much closer to one's own position in society, if only because one is in much closer contact with them. This would be necessary if only as a psychological defence mechanism; we would most of us be pretty miserable if we were permanently consumed with envy for the wealth of the late Paul Getty or the Duke of Westminster.

Thus, when Runciman asked people about the reference groups with respect to which they felt relatively deprived, the answers indicated that, say, manual workers were envious of their foreman, foremen were envious of office workers, and so on. In other words, people compared themselves one or two jumps up the ladder, in spite of the fact that they were aware of the existence of rungs in the ladder that reach far, far higher.

Similarly, when poor people living in the old slum of St Ann's, Nottingham, were asked what was 'wealth',[21] many thought that as little as £25 a week would mean wealth to them. This was little more than the average manual wage of that period (1966), £20.3 per week. Most would have been 'wealthy' if they reached £50 a week, a figure which, even in 1966, was appropriate to the average rather than the wealthy end of the middle class. (Not, of course, that £50 would leave them satisfied; presumably the reference group shifts upwards, always keeping ahead of actuality.) Again, many of the poorest people said they would be satisfied with a further £5 per week; in fact the poorer were less ambitious for improved income than the better off.

It is a long, long way from the bottom to the top in our society. The distance has perhaps been best illustrated by the two St Ann's lorry drivers overheard discussing the obvious wealth of a university professor they knew: one of them 'bet he's dragging a score a week'.[22] They would have been breathless with amazement to learn that their professor probably earned four times that salary, yet the professor, for all his salary, was still a long way short of real wealth, and would have been hurt if he had been accused of being 'rich'.

It might be thought, judging from the contributions made to public debate by the spokesmen for the poor, that people with low incomes are now much more conscious of high incomes than before. If their reference groups are higher, their relative deprivation will be greater, and the wages push will be stronger. However, a recent PEP survey that repeated certain key questions from Runciman's earlier survey has shown that no such change has taken place. Manual workers are no more likely to say that other people are doing better than themselves, and are no more likely to refer to the objectively rich, than they used to.[23] The gap between rich and poor is too wide for the poor to be able to see very far across it.

Another result of this theory is that comparatively well off people can feel genuinely deprived relative to their own reference groups, which do not include the poor. Social scientists perhaps take a wider perspective, for that is their job. Moreover, the chief reference group remaining for the middle classes, if they are not to look uncomfortably downwards, is the rich. When social scientists consider the poor, therefore, they talk about the gap between the rich and the poor. A number of social statisticians have been perplexed by the problem of summarising the extent of inequality in a society, taking into account both the richness of the rich and the poorness of the poor.[24]

The lesson from Runciman's theory of (and data on) relative deprivation is that the rich are of little direct concern to the poor. The furthest the statistician need go to seek comparison, therefore, is the average. (From this point on in the discussion, the word 'average' should be taken to refer to the situation in the middle of the range of incomes – the median – rather than a figure which tries to summarise the whole range – the mean. In fact, we shall show that there are not

so many 'average' households as one instinctively supposes.) The
condition of the poor can be expressed in terms of the average; if the
condition of the average is also expressed in terms of the rich, that is
another useful measure of inequality, but it is not of direct interest to
the poor, except in so far as the rich can be seen as a source of funds
for the poor.

This does not mean that the rich are irrelevant to a general
discussion of unfair inequality. They *are* relevant as an important end
of the chain reaction between the poor, the modest, the average, the
prosperous and the rich. This will be discussed in the final chapter of
this book. But in considering the *perceptions* of the poor, the modest
and the average are more important than the rich.

Inequality in incomes

This suggestion has some implications for the analysis of income
inequality. First, to look at the inequality suffered by the poor, it is
sufficient to compare the lowest incomes with the median, ignoring
the other half of the distribution altogether. Luckily this means that
the more complicated questions relating to ownership of wealth,
capital gains, and insurance and other fringe benefits are of much less
importance, for these complications mainly affect the top half of the
distribution. Secondly, we must look at data as far down the scale as
possible. Inland Revenue statistics are not very helpful in this
respect, as non-taxpayers are left out. Many analyses of inequality
have been concerned with the top 1 per cent, the top 10 per cent etc.,
but in no more detail than the bottom 25 per cent or even 30 per cent.

Well, what does the distribution of income among households look
like? Before looking at the graph of the distribution, it might be useful
to ponder what we would expect it to look like, and also what we feel
it ought to look like in a 'just' society. One would expect that the
'average' is somehow 'typical', i.e. that most people have about the
average income. Similarly, one would hope that a comparatively
small proportion of households would be more than a little below the
average. Translated into more technical terms one would expect a
'normal' curve (with a leftward 'skew'); and we would hope that the
upward slope of the curve (on the left) would be quite steep.
Combining what we expect and hope into a simple illustration, we get
a curve something like this:

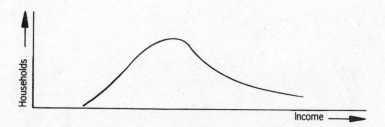

The distribution of gross household incomes, according to the 1974 *Family Expenditure Survey,* is plotted in Fig. 1.

The immediate fact that meets the eye in Fig. 1 is that the distribution is not 'normal' at all, but 'bimodal', i.e. there is not one peak, but two; and, whereas one of the peaks is where we would expect it to be, around the average, the unexpected second peak is at the very lowest end of the income distribution. Indeed, incomes in the range £12-£15 are considerably more common than any other level of income.

There is a perfectly satisfactory explanation for this – satisfactory in the sense that it provides a full explanation, though scarcely satisfactory in any moral sense. The shaded portions of the graph represent households containing no workers, most of whom are elderly households, and most of whom are mainly dependent on state incomes. Since most households with incomes below £20 are in this category, and nearly half of those between £20 and £30, the picture of income distribution is entirely revised. The lower peak is a false one consisting of pensioners, superimposed on a 'normal' distribution of incomes for other types of household. The fact that this aspect of income distribution is both unexpected and unhoped-for is the consequence of political and administrative decisions about pensions.

Comments on the remaining distribution of gross incomes are more difficult to make, as they are bound to rely on judgement as to what is a desirable scale of equality or inequality. A case can nevertheless be made that the whole distribution is too widely spread: in particular the slope of the curve below £25, which indicates the numbers of households with less than half of the average, could be much steeper; indeed, in spite of the preponderance of social security pensioners in the lower income groups, the figures indicate 1·2 million households, with a wage earner, at less than £30 p.w., and over 400,000 at less than £20. Looking at the middle ranges, we cannot say that most households tend to have an average income, but that households are

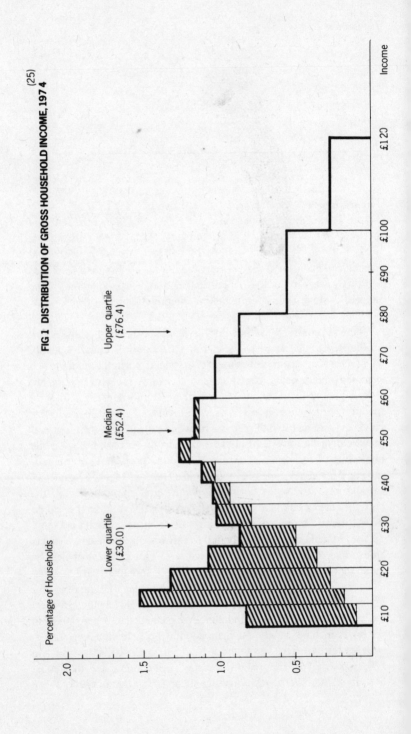

FIG 1 DISTRIBUTION OF GROSS HOUSEHOLD INCOME, 1974 (25)

spread out fairly evenly along the scale. All that we can say about the majority is that their income is between £29 and £77, roughly between 55 per cent and 147 per cent of the median.

The signs are that the distribution of income between poor and average is, if anything, becoming more, not less, unequal. Table 5 compares low incomes with average incomes between 1953-4 (the date of the first *Family Expenditure Survey*) and 1974 (the latest available).

Table 5 Changes in weekly household incomes[26]

	1953/54		1960		1968		1974	
	£	% of median	£	% of median	£	% of median	£	% of median
5th percentile	n.a.		n.a.		£7.0	26	£12.6	24
Lowest decile	n.a.		n.a.		£9.1	34	£15.7	30
15th percentile	£5.9	51	£7.2	44	£11.6	43	£19.8	38
Lower quartile	£7.9	68	£10.5	64	£17.0	63	£30.0	57
Median	£11.6	100	£16.4	100	£27.0	100	£52.4	100

In a representative group of 100 households, the income of the fifth percentile is the fifth from the bottom; the lowest decile is the income of the tenth; the fifteenth percentile is the income of the fifteenth from the bottom; the lower quartile is the income of the twenty-fifth, and the median is the income of the fiftieth.

The monetary income of all groups increased; even after allowing for the falling value of money, everyone had greater purchasing power. (The real increase of the fifteenth percentile was nearly 30 per cent.) But in the lower income groups, the increase is less: whereas the average (median) income was nearly four and a half times what it had been, the lower (fifteenth percentile) was only three and a third times what it had been. The lower income groups fell behind. In fact, if the fifteenth percentile had maintained its level relative to the median, it would have risen to £26.7 per week by 1974. The poor lost ground to the order of nearly £7 per week in twenty years.

It would be unsafe to place any great weight on the precise numerical values of these figures. The data are too fragile. We can, however, more reliably accept the general conclusion indicated. As the prosperity of the nation has increased over the past twenty years or so, the prosperity of the poorest has increased less than that of anyone else; they are now further behind the average not only in terms of the absolute gap in purchasing power, but also in the relative gap. If the differential rates of growth continued into the early years of the twenty-first century, the fifteenth percentile would reach a mere quarter of the median. Again, we can read the implication without depending on the precise accuracy of the calculation.

Part of the explanation of this trend lies in a demographic change: the proportion of the population consisting of pensioners has increased over the years,[27] swelling the ranks of the poor, but implying that not all the loss is caused by particular types of people becoming poorer.

But even leaving aside elderly households who depend on the state pension for their income, it also appears that earnings showed a tendency towards greater inequality at the bottom of the scale (Table 6).

Table 6   Changes in the wages of male manual workers[28]

	1960		1968		1975	
	£	% of median	£	% of median	£	% of median
Fifth percentile	£9.3	65	£13.6	61	£30.1	57
Lowest decile	£10.0	70	£15.1	67	£36.8	69
Lower quartile	£11.7	82	£18.2	81	£44.1	83
Median	£14.2	100	£22.4	100	£53.2	100

Although over most of the range relative pay levels have held fairly constant, the very lowest paid (fifth percentile) did considerably worse. If *their* earnings had kept pace with the others they would have reached £34.8 by 1975.

Two caveats need to be made about these analyses. Firstly, both the analysis of household incomes and of manual workers' earnings are based on gross monetary income. Changes in taxes and monetary or non-monetary benefits may have made some difference. Secondly, there are some signs that the decrease in the relative incomes of the poor took place mainly during the 1960s; the £6 limit on pay rises (set up in the summer of 1975) may also have benefited the lowest paid relatively. Nevertheless, it is difficult to argue that there is any basic effective trend towards greater equality between the poorest and those average families with whom they will compare themselves.

Meanwhile, there are some indications that the gap between the average and the top end of the income scale was closing over the 1950s and 1960s. Thus the Inland Revenue reported that their measure of equality (taken only over the top half of the range) improved fairly steadily between 1949-50 and 1969-70.[29] Other analyses of the same data reach similar conclusions.[30]

A similar conclusion is indicated by statistics which show that, while the lowest wage earners were struggling to keep up with the average manual worker, the latter was beginning to close the gap between manual and non-manual earnings (Table 7).

Table 7 Changes in mean manual and non-manual earnings[31]			
	1960	1968	1975
Manual	£14.5	£23.1	£55.7
Non-manual	£20.4	£31.7	£68.4
Manual as % of non-manual	71%	73%	81%

Analysis of the top end of the scale is more complicated than that of the bottom, since capital gains, tax avoidance (and even evasion) and fringe benefits all play a much greater part in contributing to the purchasing power of the above average, as well as taxable income. The evidence is not conclusive. Nevertheless, if it is true that the well off are slowly losing ground to the average, at the same time as the poorest are also losing ground, then the importance of using the average as the basis for comparison for the poor becomes clear. The *average* household is obtaining most of the benefits of the national economic growth – or, more precisely, the average is getting more than its previous status would have led it to expect. (Of course, the well off still get more of the increase; but they are getting less than they would expect.) The middle range is moving faster than the extremes.

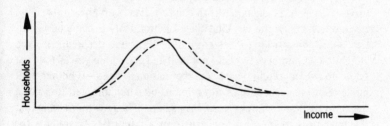

From the point of view of those in the middle ranges it is undoubtedly a 'good thing' if the degree of inequality between rich and average declines. But from the point of view of those at the bottom of the scale it can be seen that the trend is towards greater isolation. It is with those people that we are now concerned.

Historically, and within the memory of many of those active in politics and administration today, it was acceptable to divide British society into two: the haves and the have-nots. Those who were concerned with analysing or reducing this division would argue for greater rights for 'the working class', or for a diminution in 'middle-class' privileges. In the last ten years or so a new problem has been appearing, which the foregoing analysis demonstrates. If we attempt to take the working class as a whole, or typical members of it, progress towards the narrowing of differentials between them and the middle class may have been made. That is not to say, of course, that a great many undesirable distinctions do not remain. But the new point is that the working class has become too simple a concept. Within the working class there are those who are still deprived, who are not making progress in line with their more fortunate neighbours. Not only does the gap between them and the middle class remain, but the gap between them and the rest of the working class is growing wider. And since the working class is their principal source of reference groups, relative deprivation may become more acute. It will be less and less possible to accept deprivation as an inevitable aspect of an unambitious working-class background.

To state the case so clearly is perhaps to exaggerate its manifestations. Nevertheless, the theory can go some way towards explaining current anguished political debates, particularly in the area of incomes policy and 'relativities'. There are, in fact, political consequences. When the problem of inequality could be simply polarised between the working class and the middle class, arguments for social progress which, in the nineteenth century, had been philanthropic – a question of *giving* the working class a better deal – became democratic. Since the working class formed a majority, it should use the weight of its numbers to wield political and economic power to insist on a more equitable share of the national cake. Whether that movement is succeeding or not remains questionable, but it is not a question that immediately concerns us here. The new problem is that the have-nots of greatest concern form a minority. Arguments for greater social justice have again become philanthropic, and will remain so until the members of the minority can devise a source of power for themselves.

What's fair?

So far, the total income of a household has been taken as a simple indicator of that household's prosperity. We tend to classify ourselves and other people in terms of a single income figure, either for the household as a whole, or for the earnings of the head of the household. By and large, employees receive the same pay for the same task, and compare their own pay with others on this basis.

But there is, of course, a distinction between equality of *income* between households, and equality of *prosperity* through expenditure, because some households have to spend more than others to maintain the same standard of living. This may be because some people have to pay higher prices to obtain the same goods – costs of housing certainly vary substantially both between regions (and even between localities) and between tenures; variation in retail prices is probably less, although no statistics are published. A second source of inequality may be that one household has to pay for items that another household finds unnecessary: commuters, invalids and people living in isolated rural areas all have to pay extra for transport without increasing their welfare over other people. Thirdly, a large family clearly has to spend more on food, clothing, housing, indeed on practically everything, to maintain the same standard of living a small family or a single person enjoys.

If we assume, for a moment, that the Supplementary Benefit Commission knows the relationship between family composition and standard of living (i.e. if we use the S.B.C. ratios of benefit scales), then a single man taking home £30 per week has the same standard of living as a married man, with four or more children, who takes home nearly £150 per week; or, more pertinent to the poor, the family man taking home £50 has the same standard of living as a bachelor with less than £20.

Put in figures in this way, the increased costs of keeping a family may seem to be a more relevant concept than is commonly accepted in public discussion. We can see that the standard of living of a household depends as much on variations in household composition as on variations in earnings. In fact, a double standard is commonly applied, in which family size is used as a criterion in poverty analysis but not in a more general discussion of equality and inequality in society.

The consequence of such a criterion for our previous analysis of inequality is twofold. Firstly, the extremely low position of pensioners relative to the average household becomes less acute, since pensioners on the whole do not have children to support, and many do not have a spouse. Thus in Table 8 households of single persons (over half of whom are pensioners) have an income slightly better than that for families with four or more children. Even in comparison with one-child families, single people's comparative income tends to be three-quarters of the families' comparative income, although their monetary income tends to be only two-fifths of the families'. That is not to say that pensioners are well off, simply better off than a comparison of their pension with the national average income might suggest.

Table 8   Original, net, and net income per head, in households of different compositions, 1974[32]

	One adult	Man and woman	Couple & 1 child	Couple & 2 children	Couple & 3 children	2 Adults & 4+ children
Original average income	£25.76	£54.82	£64.27	£67.77	£70.92	£67.30
less average costs of housing, tax & N.I.	£8.56	£16.12	£19.06	£18.50	£18.38	£14.43
Net income	£17.20	£38.70	£45.21	£49.27	£52.34	£52.87
Number of person units*	1.00	1.63	2.00	2.37	2.74	3.29
Net income per unit	£17.20	£23.74	£22.61	£20.79	£19.10	£16.07

*Person units: persons weighted by the S.B.C. ratios.

But the second consequence of analysis by family composition is to increase the range of inequality. The monetary incomes of households with children vary very little with the number of children. It follows that when allowance for the children is made, those with many children are substantially worse off than their equivalents with few, as the decreasing net income per unit demonstrates. Hence the conclusion in *The Poor and the Poorest* that poverty could be the result of low income or large families or both.[33]

This analysis is based on the assumption that the ratios of income between households of various composition laid down by the Supplementary Benefit Commission are correct. On the other hand, there is no particular reason to believe that they are. They are based on (though they do not exactly follow) Beveridge's 1942 recommendations. They have remained virtually constant since they were first established (for the National Assistance Board) in 1948. Such small variations as have occurred from time to time cannot easily be explained.[34] In fact, in 1965 the old category for 11-15 year olds was changed, so that those aged 13-15 were given a greater benefit, but the change appears to have occurred purely within the administrative machine. For the record, the current ratios for the 'ordinary' scale are as follows:

Single person	100
Married couple	163
Any other person aged:	
Not less than 18	80
Less than 18 but not less than 16	61
,, 16 ,, 13	51
,, 13 ,, 11	42
,, 11 ,, 5	34
Less than 5	28

On the other hand, the Family Income Supplement reckons the 'target income' of a family to increase by £4.50 for each child, regardless of age. Indeed, it is probably little exaggeration to say that there are as many different sets of rules as there are different means tests.

Similarly, above the level of administratively defined indigence, we have the Family Allowance setting £1.50 per child, regardless of age; while the income tax allows upwards of £2, depending on age, for every child. In short, there is no administrative consistency; nor is there any sign that anyone has sat down to work out the cumulative effects of the various arrangements. It is clear that there is no empirical basis on which the regulations are set.

There is a strong case for thorough research into this question, and little appears to have been done. This is needed not only to ascertain how much it costs to maintain children (and a wife), but also to clarify the theoretical problems raised. It is possible to argue that a man's decision to take a wife, and the couple's decision* to have a (another) child is taken in the light of the economic facts, and that the wife or the child represents an increase in the 'happiness' obtainable on a given income. Secondly, it has been argued that to equalise net standards of living for families of various sizes would encourage excessive child-bearing (except in France, where child allowances

*Assuming it is a decision, which it is not always, especially among working-class couples. A. Cartwright [35] shows that a fifth of all mothers had had a baby they admitted they had not wanted at all; a further quarter had had one earlier than intended. Although she did not analyse these figures by social class, she does show that the working-class parents were more likely either to use no contraceptive method or to use unreliable ones, such as withdrawal.

are deliberately set high to encourage child-bearing.) What is needed, therefore, is an enquiry that covers the perceived as well as the actual costs of children, and investigates the concept of fairness in the light of one's own and one's neighbour's behaviour.

All this goes to show how little connection there is between our two standards of equality – equality of income (or of earnings) and equality of standard of living (based on family structure). They cannot be resolved until the basic structure of *earnings* is underpinned by a system of *taxes and benefits* which, as a whole, revises the distribution of the standard of living between families according to whatever principles are deemed to be fair. And that system cannot be devised until there is firm empirical knowledge about relative costs, nor until there is an informed discussion of what constitutes a 'fair' distribution.

The distinction between earnings equality and standard of living equality becomes most clear when we look at the role of women in the equation. It is well known that women are paid much less than men. The 1975 statistics for full-time earners indicate that across the whole range they earned a little more than half what the men earned, and allowances for skill level, age, or hours worked did not reduce that differential very substantially.[36] On the basis of equal earnings for equal work, 'fair pay' has rightly been demanded. Legislation now exists, but it is not yet known how far legislation can achieve the objective. The argument for equality is unanswerable.

On the other hand, most women* are either single, or married to working husbands; but many working husbands have a wife who does not work. If we were to apply the allowances for family composition used earlier, then a single woman's wages are almost 'fair' in relation to a married couple with one earner. Similarly, it is obvious that families where the wife can work are better off than families where she cannot. Thus, if inequality between men and women were reduced, inequality between different households would be more acute, according to the particular set of circumstances that allow or prevent the wife taking employment.

All this goes to show that our idea of what is fair and what is not fair depends on so wide a variety of circumstances, and so critically on our attitude towards them, that it is not possible to demonstrate that inequality is excessive merely because one set of people has a lot less

*This discussion, of course, applies *in reverse* to women who support children or other dependants by themselves.

money than another. Inequality of incomes is not *necessarily* unfair, nor would equality necessarily be fair. What *is* fair?

There are few who would be prepared to argue that total equality is in practice achievable, or even desirable, even if some universally acceptable basis for defining the scale of measurement could be adopted. As Tawney said:

> The problem of modern society is a problem of proportions, not of quantities. Peace comes not when everyone has £3 a week, but when everyone recognises that the material, objective, external arrangements of society are based on principles which they feel correspond with their subjective ideas of justice.[37]

This raises a number of questions. What is the relation between social peace and social justice? When Runciman pointed out that working-class reference groups were limited, and that the *perception* of deprivation was less than the *'objective' assessment* of it,[38] was he finding that peace is nearer at hand than justice? Tawney calls for a consensus – does the 'everyone' he mentions include middle-class social commentators, or could we argue that peace (or justice) has arrived when no one feels injustice for himself? In that case are social commentators justified in disturbing the peace (by criticising the existing stable order) in order to obtain their ideal of justice? What are we to make of the evidence that there is less social 'peace' in Sweden than in Britain, although social justice is, if anything, greater?[39]

As a society we accept that it is inevitable, necessary and even desirable that some people should have more than others. We accept, and usually approve of, most of the operations of a free market for labour, and the greater income received by some as a result of it. We accept the action of some power groups on that market (the justifiable activity of trades unions), although we may object if we think we detect the action of others (racketeering landlords). We accept that people should be paid extra if they work extra hard, or extra skilfully, or take on an extra role or responsibility, or if they have worked hard or skilfully or responsibly in the past, in order to reach an elevated position. For the most part we accept the existence of visible superiority of income or status as a symbol of authority, where the exercise of that authority appears necessary to the functioning of social institutions. If we accept that people are entitled to greater rewards, or greater incentives, or greater compensation for their effort than others, then we must of course accept that the others will get less.

Thus, before the Second World War Keynes argued for a significant degree of inequality. Nevertheless, he felt that the existing degree of inequality was unjust.[40] So, too, an opinion survey of adults in Great Britain in early 1974 found a big majority agreeing that 'People with special skills should get a lot more pay than those with no special skills', and a majority agreeing that 'Differences in pay are necessary to encourage people to work harder'; but a majority also agreed that 'There is too great a difference in this country between the pay of people in top jobs and the pay in the bottom jobs'.[41] We think that some inequality is desirable, but not as much as we have got. Maybe it is time we analysed our collective ambivalence in more detail, especially as conflicting concepts of fairness are currently in the forefront of industrial relations and political dispute.

Earlier in this chapter it was suggested that 'poverty' might be considered as that part of inequality which is unnecessary, and consequently unfair. The apparently ambivalent views described above could be resolved if we said that some inequality is necessary and desirable to make society work, but that the present extent of inequality is more than is necessary. A popular justification of inequality is based on an engineering analogy: 'You can't obtain work without a differential. A lavatory won't flush unless the cistern is above the pan.' The physical analogy is not necessarily appropriate, but it could be continued by suggesting that society uses a high-level cistern when a low-level cistern would work just as well.

In a free market prices are self-justifying: the appropriate price is the price reached in equilibrium between supply and demand. If prices are set unnecessarily high, demand will fall short of supply, and the price is forced down. How can it be said, then, that in the labour market some 'prices' are 'unnecessarily/unfairly' high and others too low? Part of the answer may be exactly the same as in any other market: if the market is no longer free, and if artificial restrictions are placed on the supply of some goods, and a flood of other goods is induced, the price ratios will be unfairly tipped in favour of the former. So, if access to some jobs is restricted, then, compared with a free market, there will be few people available to do those jobs, and a lot of people forced to accept less rewarding jobs. In this case a chain reaction sets in, resulting eventually in more people available to do certain low-level jobs than there are jobs to employ them; an excess of supply over demand then artificially lowers the price. To return to the engineering analogy, the high-level cistern has been made necessary because the pipe is partly blocked. If the blockage was removed, we would get more work out of a smaller differential.

'Equality of opportunity' is a difficult concept to discuss, and it will probably be impossible to recognise the true meritocracy when it arrives. The ideal somehow assumes that everyone has a fixed quantity of 'ability' inside him, and that he 'deserves' a reward in relation to that quantity. In practice it is difficult to see how that quantity can be measured independently of the opportunities the individual has had to develop it.

It is sometimes said that inequality is right, but that inequality of opportunity is wrong. On the other hand, if greater equality of opportunity yielded a similar degree of actual inequality as we have today, those at the bottom might not feel much better about it. But inequality of opportunity should be criticised not only *per se*, but as the means by which excessive inequality is perpetuated – the way in which access to certain jobs is restricted. If access was made easier, then the market would be freed to find more equitable price ratios. These restrictions will be discussed later in this report; few will deny that they affect racial minorities and women, and many believe that they affect people of working-class origins. The fact that some members of these groups make it to the top does not deny the existence of the restrictions; it simply indicates that they are not absolute. But it takes a big carrot and a big stick to persuade a donkey to jump over a high fence. Those who do not succeed have to be beaten with the stick, *pour encourager les autres*. Hardly fair, if the fence could be removed.

Greater fairness in jobs may therefore be a means to greater fairness in wages. It would benefit not only those who make it to better jobs, but also those who are left behind in a stronger bargaining position. On the other hand, the history of social policy is littered with means that have failed to achieve their ends – universal education and the National Health Service both seem to have done little to improve equality in education and health, for instance.* The risk is that putting faith in means, in the hope that ends will be achieved, will divert attention from the ends themselves. Why not a *direct* attack on unequal incomes? Perhaps equality of opportunity would be one of its consequences!

*See Chapters 4 and 7.

Increasing taxes and benefits may be one way of pressing that attack. But the distribution of original incomes is also worth tackling, partly because the knowledge that Lord X has a gross income of £100,000 may be more harmful than the fact that he is able to spend only £10,000 after tax, and partly because the wasted £90,000 represents wages that could be paid to a large number of workers. There is one sign, however, of a changing attitude to earnings differentials which, if firmly established, might have a considerable effect in the medium and long term.

From the analytical point of view, there is little doubt that the arithmetic of multiplication and division is the most appropriate way of examining inequality, pay differentials, pay rises and so on. X earns *twice* as much as Y and a *third* as much as Z. The cost of living has risen *15 per cent.* ABC Ltd has *doubled* its wages bill. In consequence, it is seen to be 'fair' if all workers receive the same *percentage* increase. It is fair, if the present distribution is seen to be fair. But an increase of 10 per cent gives £500 to the £5,000 man, and only £100 to the £1,000 man. If we changed to the arithmetic of addition and subtraction, then a 'fair' increase in wages might be £250 to each man. If we continue to use addition and subtraction arithmetic, the differential (of £4,000) would be seen to be maintained, but as all earnings increased over the years, that differential would become less painful.

There is some evidence that a move in this direction would be acceptable. For instance, when a sample of people were asked how much more income they felt they 'needed', the better-off did ask for more absolutely, but less relatively (Table 9).

Table 9 Increased income demanded, by actual income[42]
(weekly figures)

	£9-13	£17-21	£25-29	£33-40	£50 and over
Median absolute increase	£4	£6	£8	£9	£12½
Median relative increase	36%	32%	30%	25%	20%

This suggests that the better-off might accept less than they would be entitled to if constant percentages were the rule. Similarly, it appears that satisfaction with a pay rise is statistically more related to its absolute size than to its size as a percentage of previous earnings.[43] A compromise between ratios and intervals may be most appropriate. For example, the most successful of the phases of the 1972-4 pay code (phase II) was based on the formula '£1 plus 4%'. The

1975/76 pay limit (£6) was a fixed figure for all; whereas the 1976/77 pay limit again uses a mixture. (It could be argued, on the other hand, that all this evidence applies to static or short-term situations, and that in the longer term fixed-sum increases would collapse.) The arithmetic of multiplication and division may continue to be necessary for calculating and statistics, but addition and subtraction may be preferable for public discussion. It will have no magical results, but it should help.

So far, this chapter has concentrated on inequality of income. But it is also useful to look briefly at inequality of capital. On a superficial view inequality of wealth is simple and well known. There are some people whose wealth is, quite literally, unimaginable even to the highest paid people who depend on an earned income. There are very few such people, who hold so much wealth that they might almost be considered to hold all the real riches. The following figures, inaccurate as they are admitted to be (probably in underestimating the degree of concentration), show it all pretty clearly.[44]

1 per cent of the population own	29 per cent of the wealth					
5 per cent ,, ,,	,,	,,	53 per cent	,,	,,	,,
10 per cent ,, ,,	,,	,,	69 per cent	,,	,,	,,
25 per cent ,, ,,	,,	,,	93 per cent	,,	,,	,,

In considering deprivation, however, we want to think about people at the very bottom, not the very top. It is clear from the figures above that virtually all the wealth will have been accounted for long before anywhere near all the people have been; conversely, a very large proportion of the population must have no wealth at all. It would be nice to know at what stage this nothing-at-all lifts off the floor to become modest savings; how modest savings passes through a transition towards a bit of capital; and where a bit of capital reaches the point of wealth. Unfortunately very little is known about the ownership of savings/capital/wealth at the lower end of the spectrum, and virtually nothing about what difference such ownership makes to people's lives either in the normal course of events or, more importantly, in a crisis.

If capital is looked at from the point of view of its effects on people's lives, then it may be reasonable to adopt a simpler approach than that necessary for economists, political theorists or theoretical sociologists. Many kinds of capital can reasonably be ignored. The individual citizen's theoretical share in the nationalised industries and in the capital assets of the National Health Service need not be counted as being his own, as he does not possess the right to dispose of them. Similarly, his rights to a future National Insurance pension are of little consequence to his working life, with the important exception that they make it less necessary for him to retain his savings against old age; private or occupational insurance schemes come into the same category, unless they are realisable. So from the man in the street's point of view the important items are, first, liquid or semi-liquid savings, and, secondly, the capital cushion provided by owner-occupation of a house.

Although there is no good detailed information on who has how much savings, a general question asked in a recent PEP survey gives a fair indication of the distribution. Only one-quarter of the population can count on a nest-egg of £500 or more. Nearly a half have less than £100, and nearly a quarter have nothing at all. But, of course, the distribution is quite different when the different social classes are looked at separately (Table 10).

Table 10 Savings in different social grades[45]

	Total	Managerial/ professional	Clerical	Skilled manual	Semi/un- skilled
	(per cent)	(per cent)	(per cent)	(per cent)	(per cent)
None at all	23	7	12	22	38
Under £100	25	13	25	28	27
£100–£499	26	23	28	30	23
£500 or more	25	58	36	20	12

Presumably the difference in savings between the top and bottom of the scale is due largely to differences in the availability of income after essential expenditure, as well as on the possibility of inheritance of small or large sums. In the middle of the scale differences in the individual's personal propensity to save income on the one hand, or to 'blow' small windfalls on the other, must also play their part,[46] although the manual worker's relative uncertainty about his income stability must also have an external effect on his ability to plan his savings (see p. 134).

Whatever the reasons, manual workers, and particularly low-status manual workers, are unlikely to have a nest-egg large enough to pay off a single unforeseen debt – the sort of item that better-off people may have been able to insure against anyway. For a more serious, or longer-term, emergency even £500 is small enough, but that is a level rarely reached by those who – as we shall see in later chapters – are most likely to come to need it.

Apart from liquid savings, there is another widely held form of capital, which, in theory, constitutes a cushion against calamity – the owner-occupied home. To the extent that the market value of the home exceeds the size of the mortgage (through repayment of the debt, and/or through inflation) this represents a real capital asset. Whether it can be used in an emergency is another question. The owner-occupier must either obtain another mortgage or sell. It is doubtful whether mortgages can be obtained when the owner is in trouble – certainly not an unskilled worker facing a period of unemployment. Second mortgages are probably more useful for increasing current prosperity, or at most tiding over a small temporary problem, than for saving an already difficult situation. Selling out necessitates both sacrificing the home, a major step, and finding rented accommodation as an alternative – probably not from the council, unless on strictly housing grounds. We do not know how often owner-occupiers do draw on this capital asset, but it is certainly not easy. Less than 10 per cent of owner-occupiers move in any year; of those, only 13 per cent move into rented housing.[47] So only about 1 per cent of all owner-occupiers move into rented housing, many of them for reasons that have little or nothing to do with capital realisation. In any case, those who are most likely to need the capital asset of a house are least likely to possess it (Table 11).

Table 11 Owner-occupation in different social groups[48]

Managerial/ professional	Clerical	Skilled manual	Semi-skilled	Un-skilled
78%	58%	46%	30%	23%

In summary it is obvious that the possession of real wealth makes an enormous difference to the current prosperity and future security of a small minority of people. But even if this is left on one side, and only commonly available forms of capital are considered, there remains a very real and important degree of inequality.

NOTES

1 According to the Department of Employment and Productivity's *British Labour Statistics, Historical Abstract, 1886-1968,* H.M.S.O., 1971, the purchasing power of the pound in 1914 was about 4.8 times its 1968 value. The current series of retail price

indices (published in the *Department of Employment Gazette*) shows the 1975 value to be about 0.39 of its 1962 value. The ratio 1914:1975 is therefore 12.3:1.

2 The 1906 figures come from *British Labour Statistics, op. cit.*, and the 1975 figures from the Department of Employment's *New Earnings Survey 1975*, H.M.S.O.

3 Television ownership does fall off slightly among the very poorest households, but three-quarters even of the lowest income group nevertheless possess one – possibly a very ancient model:

Under £12	*£12-15*	*£15-25*	*£25-45*	*£45-100*	*Over £100*
77%	82%	90%	94%	97%	99%

(Department of Employment, *Family Expenditure Survey 1974*, H.M.S.O., 1975.)

4 P. Townsend, 'Poverty as Relative Deprivation', in D. Wedderburn (ed.) *Poverty, Inequality and Class Structure*, Cambridge University Press, 1974. Townsend was quoting the standard set out by Rowntree for his study of poverty in 1899 – see note 9. It may be of interest to compare this with the current standard laid down by the Supplementary Benefits Commission. The quantities are not much different, although the quality is no longer set down as substandard:

Overcoat or raincoat	1
Cardigan	1
Dress (a jumper and skirt or trousers count as one dress)	2
Stockings or tights	3 pairs
Shoes	2 pairs
Slips	2
Vests	2
Pants	2
Brassières	2
Corset or girdle	1
Nightwear	2

5 R. Titmuss, *Income Distribution and Social Change*, Allen & Unwin, 1962.

6 A review of the evidence on inequality is to be found in A. B. Atkinson, 'Poverty and Income Inequality in Britain', in D. Wedderburn (ed.), *op. cit.*

7 J. L. Nicholson, 'The distribution and redistribution of income in the United Kingdom', in D. Wedderburn (ed.) *op. cit.*

8 If the median income were always twice the lowest decile, and half the highest decile, then an annual compound growth rate of 15 per cent would mean that one-tenth of incomes would be below the 5-year-ago-median; zero growth would mean that one-half of incomes would be below the 5-year-ago-median; a 13 per cent annual *decline* in real incomes would mean that nine-tenths of incomes would be below the 5-year-ago-median.

These figures are intended merely to illustrate the potential importance of dynamics to the analysis of incomes inequality. Objectively, there is no reason for preferring the 5-year-ago-median as the bench-mark; the 10-year-ago-median, the 5-year-ago-lower-quartile or any other point would give quite different figures. What *is* certain is that if memory of the recent past affects the 'social norm', then a slowing of growth increases the extent of poverty, unless the limited growth is channelled to the worst-off.

9 B. S. Rowntree, *Poverty, A Study of Town Life*, Macmillan, 1901.

10 B. S. Rowntree, *Poverty and Progress*, Longmans, 1941.

11 B. S. Rowntree and G. R. Lavers, *Poverty and the Welfare State*, Longmans, 1951.

12 B. Abel-Smith and P. Townsend, *The Poor and the Poorest*, Bell, 1965.

13 This measure was not offered as 'an objective or an ideal definition of poverty – though their work was subsequently misinterpreted as such.' See footnote 41 to P. Townsend, 'Poverty as Relative Deprivation', in D. Wedderburn (ed.), *op. cit.*

14 Abel-Smith and Townsend, *op. cit.*, Tables 3 and 12.

15 The U.S. measure is described and defended by M. Orshansky. See 'Counting the Poor; another look at the poverty profile', *Social Security Bulletin, Vol. 28*, 1965; 'Who was Poor in 1966', *Research and Statistics Note*, U.S. Dept of Health, Ed. and Welfare, Dec. 1967; and 'How Poverty is Measured', *Monthly Labour Review*, Feb. 1969.

16 A detailed critique of subsistence line measures comes in P. Townsend's 'Poverty as Relative Deprivation', in D. Wedderburn (ed.), *op. cit.*, and elsewhere.

17 When the 1964-66 Labour Government made comparatively generous increases in Assistance/Benefit rates, the number of 'poor' did go up. See K. Lafitte, 'Income Deprivation', in R.

Holman (ed.), *Socially Deprived Families in Britain*, Bedford Square Press, 1971.

18 D.H.S.S., *Social Security Statistics 1974*. In detail the ratio of S.B. rates to average manual earnings reached a peak in 1966, and has been slowly declining ever since. See Chapter 2, p. 55.

19 Absolute poverty resulting directly in death may not have been as common in this country as our historical image may suggest, although it is difficult to measure. Starving people do not usually die directly of lack of food. The fluctuations in mortality mentioned as one of the consequences of absolute poverty seem to have been more common in France than in England. See P. Laslett, *The World We Have Lost*, Methuen, 1965. But it is not important to our discussion to know when absolute poverty gave way to relative poverty. The point is that absolute poverty, if it exists, needs to be eliminated; relative poverty needs to be acted upon, but the aim is not elimination.

20 W. G. Runciman, *Relative Deprivation and Social Justice*, Rout-ledge & Kegan Paul, 1966. The theory itself had been formulated by earlier sociologists, but it was Runciman who gave it its practical meaning.

21 K. Coates and R. Silburn, *Poverty, the Forgotten Englishmen*, Penguin Books, 1970.

22 *Ibid.*

23 W. W. Daniel, *The PEP Survey on Inflation*, PEP Broadsheet No. 553, 1975.

24 Both Townsend and Atkinson discuss this difficulty in their essays in D. Wedderburn, *op. cit.*

25 Department of Employment, *Family Expenditure Survey 1974, op. cit.* The percentage of households having an income in a given range has been divided by the number of £s in that range. Thus the height of each column represents approximately the percentage of all households with an income of a given £1 range. The *area* of each column is proportional to the percentage of households in the whole range.

26 Figures for 1953-4: D.E.P., *British Labour Statistics, op. cit.* Figures for 1974: *F.E.S. 1974, op. cit.*

27 Between 1951 and 1971 the dependency ratio of pensioners (persons of pensionable age per 1,000 population of working age) increased from 212 to 272. See Central Statistical Office, *Social Trends, No. 4*, H.M.S.O., 1973.

28 Figures for 1960: D.E.P., *British Labour Statistics, op. cit.* Figures for 1975: *New Earnings Survey, op. cit.*

29 Board of Inland Revenue, *Incomes Survey 1969-70* (H.M.S.O., 1972), Chapter II.

30 See A. B. Atkinson, 'Poverty and Income Inequality in Britain', in D. Wedderburn (ed.), *op. cit.*

31 As note 28.

32 *Family Expenditure Survey 1974:* Children are assumed to be randomly distributed between the ages of 0 and 15.

33 Abel-Smith and Townsend, *op. cit.*

34 See B. Abel-Smith and C. Bagley, 'The Problem of Establishing Equivalent Standards of Living for Families of Different Composition', in P. Townsend (ed.), *The Concept of Poverty,* Heinemann, 1970.

35 A. Cartwright, *Parents and Family Planning Services,* Routledge & Kegan Paul, 1970.

36 *New Earnings Survey, op. cit.*

37 R. H. Tawney, quoted in D. Wedderburn (ed.), *op. cit.*

38 W. G. Runciman, *op. cit.*

39 R. Scase, 'Relative Deprivation: a comparison of English and Swedish manual workers', in D. Wedderburn (ed.), *op. cit.* This indicates greater subjective deprivation in Sweden, in that reference groups are set higher, and workers are more conscious of the extent of differentials above them. On the other hand *actual* differentials seemed no more, and probably less, than in Britain.

40 Reported by R. Titmuss, *op. cit.*

41 P. Fish and D. Jackson, 'Pay Policy and Inflation: What Britain Thinks', in *New Society,* 7 Feb. 1974. These three results quoted on their own may suggest that respondents agreed with everything the interviewer said to them. On the other hand, two other statements in the same battery (one left wing, one right wing) were rejected by a majority of the sample.

42 Taken from M. Abrams, 'Subjective Social Indicators', in *Social Trends, No. 4, 1973.* All the figures are approximate, especially the very last (in brackets), as the median actual income in each group is not known.

43 W. W. Daniel, *The PEP Survey on Inflation, op. cit.*

44 C.S.O., *Social Trends,* 1975

45 Unpublished data from the survey reported in W. W. Daniel, *The PEP Survey on Inflation, op. cit.* The 'social grade' used here is

based on the I.P.A. scale: AB, C_1, C_2, DE. In answer to these questions 6 per cent of the sample would not say whether or not they had any savings, and 15 per cent would not say how much. These refusals are assumed to have been at random within social grade, but they reduce the reliability of the percentages shown.

46 W. G. Runciman, 'Occupational Class and the assessment of economic inequality', in D. Wedderburn, *op. cit.*

47 Central Statistical Office, *Social Trends, No. 5,* 1974.

48 O.P.C.S., *General Household Survey 1973.* H.M.S.O., 1976.

2 Income and social security

Income is, of course, a key measure of inequality. It may even be the main one, if it can be argued that most other aspects of inequality either stem from, or result in, a low income. On the other hand, it is not sufficient to define the deprived simply in terms of low income, since this would ignore those with a slightly higher income but a series of other problems.

Analysis of the distribution of incomes has already appeared, in the previous chapter, to provide material for the general discussion of inequality. In this chapter the focus is more specifically on the sources of income for those at a low level of living, from the point of view of the social security system. For this purpose, provisions by the state for waiving or reducing the charges for various goods or services will be regarded as the equivalent of income, since they have the effect of releasing money from the household budget for other expenditure. On the other hand, earnings are really considered as a fixed element in this chapter; the problem of low wages is considered under the heading of employment (Chapter 5).

The Social Security system is, of course, immensely complicated. That in itself calls for some discusssion later in the chapter, but it also makes it necessary to preface any discussion with the admission that it is virtually impossible to comment on 'the system' as a whole, as opposed to specific aspects of it as they affect specific groups of people. Apart from the difficulty for a person not versed in the law to comprehend the whole, very little information indeed is available to relate different aspects one to the other.

Supplementary Benefit

The most important single provision, if not in numbers of payments then in terms of preventing total indigence, is Supplementary Benefit.

At the end of 1974 (Table 12) there were nearly 2.7 million regular weekly payments current.[1]

Table 12   Regular weekly payments of Supplementary Benefit, November 1974

		per cent
Supplementary pensions	1,807,000	67
Unemployed	301,000	11
Sick and disabled	260,000	10
Women with dependent children	245,000	9
Others	66,000	2
TOTAL	2,679,000	

The total figure represents an increase of 36 per cent over the end of 1964 (1,961,000). This is explained partly by an increase in the number of pensioners since then, and also by the growing social acceptability of receiving state assistance. Thus there was a huge leap (of 25 per cent) in the number of regular weekly payments at the end of 1966,[2] when the name 'National Assistance' was dropped in preference to 'Supplementary Benefit' precisely to avoid the slur of going to charity. (The change of name symbolised a number of other important changes at that time, which would, no doubt, have had an effect even without the change of name.) The greatest increase over the ten-year period was among women with dependent children – from 95,000 to 245,000 – again at least partly explained by a change in take-up rates as well as by an increasing number of such families. It is therefore difficult to use these statistics to look at variations in low levels of income, since the increases at least partially indicate an improvement in the incomes of many households.

Actually, 1973 was the only year for a long time that saw a drop in the number of S.B. claimants. Some of this drop was caused by an easing of unemployment rates, but most of it was caused by changes in rules relating to non-S.B. provisions. Thus, the number of Supplementary Pensions dropped as some of the pensioners benefited from the new rent rebates; similarly many National Insurance claimants benefited from a more generous medium-term scale.

The S.B. basic rates set from November 1976 are £20.65 for a married couple and £12.70 for a single householder, with additional rates for children of various ages (see p. 39). The system is that a claimant's and his dependants' 'needs' are set according to these rates, plus the rent on their accommodation (unless this is deemed 'unreasonable'). If their income is less than their needs, then Supplementary Benefit makes up the difference in full.

In looking at changes in S.B. rates over the years we must

distinguish between their monetary value, their real value (in relation to the purchasing power of the pound), and what we may call their social value (in relation to the average earnings of more fortunate households). Their monetary value increased from 1948 to end-1975 nearly ninefold, but that comparison in itself does not tell us very much.[3] In the same period, however, retail prices increased to three and a half times their 1948 rate, so that the real value of benefits went up two and a half times. Even if we allow for the fact that the budgets of poor households, with their concentration on food, may have been harder hit by inflation than the average, there has clearly been a substantial increase in the real value of benefits. The increase in real value has been fairly constant, if sporadic. On four occasions (in 1966, 1969, 1973 and 1975) a new rate has been set slightly lower than the real value of the previous rate at its introduction. And the new rate set for November 1976 will again be slightly less valuable than the November 1975 rate, unless inflation slows down remarkably.

But it has been argued in Chapter 1 that absolute measures of purchasing power are not so relevant to the poor as measures of their relation with average members of the society in which they live. Looked at in the long term, S.B. rates have kept up with average earnings of male manual workers – in fact their 'social value' at the 1975 revision was almost exactly the same as in 1948. The general tendency is, therefore, for the rates to maintain a fairly constant relation with average male manual earnings. On the other hand, this has been subject to ebbs and flows – in 1965 the rate was set as high as 23 per cent above its 1948 social value, but it dropped slightly in seven of the ten following reviews. Thus we have seen a period of relative decline in the social value of the S.B. rates, although the government has resolved to index them in relation to earnings in future.

The most striking aspect of the distribution of S.B. among different types of claimant (see p. 54) is the fact that two-thirds of the recipients are pensioners on Supplementary Pensions. This is in accord with the general conclusion that old people, who form 16 per cent of the population of the country,[4] have far more than their fair share of all the problems associated with deprivation. Looking at these numbers the other way round, the official figure for the proportion of pensioners receiving Supplementary Benefit is 25 per cent.[5] If the number of pensioners living at or below S.B. levels but not claiming it are added in, the figure would be about 35 per cent.[6] Unless a pensioner gets help from his family, or goes into an

institution, or during his working life has succeeded in securing a
good private or occupational pension, there is a good chance of his
income depending in the end not on his pension but on Supplementary
Benefit. Clearly, the overlap is sufficient for the relation between
pensions and Supplementary Benefit to be questioned; or, more
generally, the relation between insurance and welfare provisions.

Supplementary Benefit and National Insurance
Income entitlement is very similar, whether based on National
Insurance payments, or on Supplementary Benefits (Table 13).

Table 13 Income entitlement
(from November 1976):

	For the unemployed		For pensioners (under 80)	
	N.I.	S.B.	N.I.	S.B.
Man, or lone woman	£12.90	£12.70 (+ rent)	£15.30	£15.70 (+ rent)
Dependent wife	£8.00	£7.95	£9.20	£9.15
(plus further benefits for dependent children)				

Although in practice the sums of money available are very similar,
and always have been, in theory the two systems operate on quite
different principles: the pension and unemployment benefit are based
on insurance principles, and S.B. on welfare principles. On the
welfare principle a household is given simply what it 'needs', but on
the insurance principle a pensioner* receives what he is 'entitled to',
depending on his contributions. If he failed to keep up sufficient
contributions during his working life, he would receive less than the
flat rate; conversely, by making slightly higher contributions, he
would receive a graduated pension ($36\frac{1}{2}$ per cent of pensions were thus
increased by an average of 27p each in 1974);[7] or, by deferring
retirement beyond the normal age, he could receive an increment (26
per cent of pensions, average increment 49p).[8] Depending on the
contributions, the pension is fixed on the one condition that the
recipient has in fact retired—beyond the age of 70 for men and 65 for
women even that condition is dropped.

To the extent that the fixed pension enables the pensioner to reap
the benefits of any other savings or insurance he may have accumu-
lated during his working life, it is to be applauded. But it is fixed so
low that a huge number of pensioners who were unable to insure,

*The rest of this discussion is based on pensioners, but could also be applied to the sick
and disabled, the unemployed and so on.

privately or occupationally, are dependent on a supplement. They are no better off than the 100,000 old people without any pension, dependent entirely on Supplementary Benefit, although they may feel a greater self-respect. Moreover, the income from an old person's savings or independent pension must exceed his rent before he or she receives any real benefit. But the great majority of occupational pensions, for example, are too small to have this effect.

The principle underlying insurance is that people should, in a sense, save up for their pension in advance through their contributions. When the welfare state as we know it was launched after the Second World War, the intention was that National Insurance would cover most situations adequately, and Assistance would be used in emergency to fill the odd gap. We can now see that the advocacy of insurance as the underlying principle was a means of persuading moderate or conservative opinion of the reasonable nature of the scheme; the state was not so much interfering with the structure of society as setting itself up as a giant and altruistic version of the Prudential.

Now that we have had the system for over twenty-five years, most of us have forgotten the importance of the insurance principle; indeed in practice it has suffered fairly heavy abuse in the constant adjustment of benefits to meet cases of special need, and in its underpinning finance. Yet in a recently proposed wholesale revision of the pension system, the insurance principle was not only preserved but extended to absurd lengths. The state's interference is surely justified only if it equalises risks to a greater extent than a private scheme could afford to; yet in the proposed State Reserve Scheme, a woman's pension would be less than a man's (even assuming equal salaries at work) on the purely actuarial basis that, as her retiring age is five years earlier, and she tends to live longer, she would make fewer contributions and draw benefit for a longer time! Women were to suffer financially for their longevity, as well as living on their own in widowhood.[9] Fortunately, that proposal has been killed by the results of two general elections. But even its successor, vast improvement though it is, remains recognisably linked to the insurance principle, in its emphasis on contributions and in the long lead-in period before it can become fully operational.

We have, therefore, two systems, both for pensioners and for other types of state dependant, run in parallel at roughly the same level of benefit. When the two were instituted after the war, the distinction was made between those who had earned their benefit (National Insurance) and those who had not (Supplementary Benefit, in those days known as National Assistance). At the time it was felt that the moral overtones of this distinction were useful; it is now felt (officially) that there should be no moral distinction, but the continuation of the administrative distinction perpetuates the moral one in the public view. Moreover, whenever the insurance entitlement is (x), the S.B. entitlement is usually about (x+rent), so that unless there is some third independent source of income, a substantial proportion of National Insurance beneficiaries have to apply for Supplementary Benefit anyway. The converse is that those who do have some small independent source of income are no better off either. Quite apart from the question of the size of these benefits, the system clearly requires a rethink. In the course of that rethink the insurance principle could usefully be finally abandoned. The use of general taxation to effect a transfer of benefits between generations, or between groups in different need, is already well established. We pay for our children's schooling, etc., on the basis that our parents paid for ours. Why can we not pay our parents' pensions, therefore, on the understanding that our children will pay for ours? Moreover, the principle of tying a particular expense to a particular source of revenue is wholly rejected in all other fields, in spite of loud objections, for instance from motorists (who argue that revenue from the road fund tax should be earmarked for expenditure on roads).

Supplementary Benefit and the time dimension

What can concretely be said about the level of living of those on Supplementary Allowances or Pensions, other than that most people would rather not live on that amount? One thing that can be said in its favour is that the level is not much below that experienced by families with many children and/or very low wages[10] That does not say much for the families or their wages, but from the Supplementary Beneficiaries' point of view it would be worse otherwise.

It has never been clear exactly how it was decided at what level National Assistance rates (from which Supplementary Benefit rates were derived) should be set. Since N.A./S.B. rates have always been very close to National Insurance rates, it seems reasonable to assume that they were fixed on that basis. It can be argued that National Insurance rates in turn were originally set at a level believed to be just acceptable in the short term, but increasingly uncomfortable in the medium and long term, providing a strong incentive for the unemployed to find another job quickly. If this train of argument is accepted, then the S.B. level, too, must be a short-term expedient. In the light of that intention, look at the actual length of time that claimants of various types have been continuously dependent (Table 14).

Table 14 Length of time in receipt of Supplementary Benefit, November 1974[11]

	All S.B. pensioners	Unemployed with NI	w/out NI*	Sick etc. with NI	w/out NI*	Women with dependent children
	%	%	%	%	%	%
Less than 6 months	4	83	52	24	16	22
6 months, less than 1 year	4	15	9	9	6	13
1 year but less than 2	8	2	11	11	9	17
2 years but less than 5	22	∅	18	27	19	28
5 years but less than 10	37	∅	8	21	19	15
10 years or over	25	—	2	9	32	5

*The lack of N.I. benefits among many unemployed, sick and disabled is partly a consequence of their greater length of time out of work, dependent on S.B.
φ=more than 0 but less than 0.5 per cent)

Of the unemployed Supplementary Beneficiaries (both groups combined), 40 per cent have been on S.B. for over a year; 48 per cent of unsupported mothers, 65 per cent of the sick or disabled, and 84 per cent of pensioners have been dependent for over two years. A quarter of the pensioners and nearly a third of one of the sick and disabled categories have been dependent for over ten years. When you come to think about it, how can anyone have expected any different? Yet they have to live at a level set as an emergency stopgap, in spite, in the latter cases, of the further problems of extreme old age or extreme incapacity. And, it will be argued later in this chapter, it is over time that living on a very low income becomes so difficult.

This highly critical view of the problem is not quite fair, for in the past couple of years the thin end of a very important wedge has been inserted into the S.B. system. Until October 1973 there was a provision for a 'long-term addition' to the scale rates of pensioners and those who had been in receipt of benefit for over two years (except for the unemployed). This addition was of the princely sum of 60p (85p for those aged over 80) for the whole household. In October 1973 a new long-term scale was introduced, giving extra allowances of £1.00 to a single householder and £1.20 for a couple. In July 1974 the gap was widened to £2.00 for a single person and £2.70 for a couple: representing an improvement of about 25 per cent and 20 per cent respectively over the 'ordinary' rate. This relative improvement has been maintained at subsequent reviews. At the same time N.I. benefits for the old and/or unemployable have also been increased relative to unemployment provisions.

This is an important, if not a large, step in the right direction, for it indicates that those who are not expected to work at all are to be treated on their own merits, not tied to a system designed with the short-term unemployed in mind. On the other hand, if the two are to be treated independently, it can be argued the gap could be much wider. (It can, of course, be argued in the opposite direction, that the wider the gap, the more unfair on those who do not benefit from it.)[12] Secondly, it is not clear why those who are not expected to work (sick, disabled, unsupported mothers) but are not old, have to wait two long and painful years before they qualify – effectively excluding about half of them from the increased benefit.[13]

Supplementary Benefit and the incentive to work

Very similar arguments pertain to the discussion of work incentives. Undoubtedly, one of the key historical criteria for setting S.B. so low is that it should be set at least as low as, if not slightly below, the standard of living of those in work. This brings in questions of incentives, and of fairness. As far as incentives are concerned, the idea is to encourage those on S.B. to remove themselves from dependence on the state by working, and to discourage those already working from allowing themselves to become dependent on the state. The evidence at present suggests that the 'workshy' (although they undoubtedly do exist) are rare;[14] on the other hand, this does not prove that if it was more profitable to depend on the state, more people might not put two and two together and manoeuvre themselves out of the workforce. Still, most of the currently unemployed are not voluntarily so, and it does seem hard on them that they should risk suffering serious poverty for the benefit of a few malingerers. Nevertheless, by comparison with other groups of S.B. claimants, most of them are on hard times for a relatively short period (see p. 59); it would not be unreasonable to give them a strong motive for seeking a job, *if the problem of unemployment itself were tackled effectively* (see Chapter 5).

But, viewed in the context of S.B. claimants as a whole, we can see the question of employment incentives as being largely irrelevant. Table 12 (p. 54) shows that only 9 per cent of all S.B. dependants are considered by the Commission to be in the market for employment

– and the Commission can hardly be accused of being lax in its categorisations. Most of the rest are retired (67 per cent), sick or disabled (10 per cent) or women with dependent children (9 per cent). All these people are unable to work, and as a society we do not feel they should be made to work; and they often have personal problems of their own which make indigence harder to bear. Yet until recently they were expected to live on an income barely above a scale intended to 'punish' or at least to discourage the workshy.

In fact, for this majority of state-dependent people, the system intended to provide a strong work incentive actually deters them from making what contribution to the economy they might be capable of. Pensioners (under the age of 70) are actually required to retire before they can receive their pension; but many pensioners, sick or disabled people, and unsupported mothers may be capable of working part time without serious personal problems arising. (Pensioners working part time do not lose much of their N.I. pension, and the rules on this have recently been relaxed. But they do lose most of their S.B. pension.) They would like to raise their standard of living; they would obtain social and psychological advantages from working; but the means test associated with S.B. means that (apart from the first £4) they would have to put in 10, 20, or even more hours of work a week for no net reward, before any material advantage could accrue.

The conflict is well illustrated by the position of mothers with young children (Table 15). Among mothers with husbands living with them, only 20 per cent are in any way economically active, and a mere 5 per cent work full time (more than thirty hours per week). That suggests that our society accepts that mothers of children under school age are entitled to devote their attention to them. But for unsupported mothers a very serious conflict arises between opposing pressures: between the need to care for their children like other mothers and the need to go out to work.

The strength of the latter pressure is sufficient to persuade one-and-

Table 15 Economic status of women with dependent children aged 0-4[15]

	Wives in married couples (per cent)	Widowed, divorced, separated and single mothers (per cent)
Economically inactive	80	69
Work part time*	15	16
Work full time (30 hrs+)	5	15

*Includes economically active, but unemployed.

a-half times as many unsupported mothers to work at all, and three times as many of them to work full time. Even so two-thirds of them are unable to get out to work; and the fact that they are unable to yield to this pressure does not mean that they do not feel the conflict it causes.

Old people, sick and disabled people, and unsupported mothers are not that difficult to identify, and to distinguish from those who are otherwise unemployed. In fact they are identified, and receive some favour from the S.B. Commission. But since incentives arguments do not apply to them (or do we believe that generosity would encourage them to grow old, to become sick, to desert their husbands or to get pregnant?), their allowances could be made quite independent of the unemployment benefit rates, and the two-year qualifying term could be relaxed.

The final incentive argument suggests that benefits should be kept low to encourage people to take independent measures to insure themselves against hard times. To this there are four responses. First, if the state accepts half the responsibility for social insurance, why should it not accept it all? Secondly, the means test often makes it necessary to insure oneself *heavily* to obtain any net advantage. Thirdly, the fact that so many people have failed to insure themselves adequately – for whatever reasons – suggests that the incentive effect is not sufficiently powerful. Fourthly, there are important risks against which it is virtually impossible to insure: against unemployment, for example, or against sickness for those already in poor health.

The alternative justification for setting all S.B. rates at or below the standard of living of the lowest wage earners involves concepts of fairness. Is it fair (or will low-wage earners *feel* that it is fair) that they should remain at a low standard of living while contributing to the work effort and the economy, while there are those who do not work (however justifiably) who are better off than they are? There is undoubtedly jealousy, even at present, between those who work for low wages and those who 'shirk it' on the state. It is probably this jealousy that gives rise to feelings of shame and reluctance to apply for benefit; and the possibility of greater jealousy certainly makes the radical improvement in benefits to unsupported mothers, and at least the less obviously sick and disabled (if not to pensioners), more difficult to justify. On the other hand, might not an overt and deliberate declaration by the government that these people have special problems and special entitlements prevent an increase in jealousy? Or even eliminate the jealousy that exists, by clarifying the distinction between unemployment and other problems?

It is therefore rather difficult to justify the present level of benefits to people on the poverty line by purely rational arguments. Nor need it be argued that there is not enough money in the Treasury to pay for increases, for, in the long term at least, if the intention were firm enough, the resources could be found. It appears that this is one of the areas where government feels it to be its duty to spend the least that public opinion will tolerate. This is a philosophy that has long been powerful in many state activities – that we should accept a much lower standard from the state than we would expect in private enterprise. The philosophy of parsimony extends right down from important issues like social security to lesser matters like dreary doctors' surgeries and the rule that civil servants may not drink office tea unless they provide their own cups!

But in some fields we can see that the state is beginning to spend not the least, but the most, that public opinion will tolerate. Thus public funds are being used to provide the very best motorways, important new hospitals, and so on, that money will buy. Let us hope that this new philosophy will soon apply to the dependants of the state.

Living on a low income

What sort of a budget does Supplementary Benefit provide, or what, for that matter, is it like living at or around the S.B. level on low earnings? Probably the benefit is just about enough to live adequately on, if members of the household include both a *first-class housekeeper* and a *first-class domestic lawyer*.

Let us first consider the housekeeping aspects of the problem. Clearly, the more limited the budget, the less scope there is for variation or mistakes, and the more important a 'virtuous' as well as skilful housekeeper becomes. On only £10 a week a mistake costing £1 can be fatal; moreover, at such low levels of living, the proportion of the budget spent on essential housekeeping is much higher than among average households, where a proportion is available for non-necessities. The poorest have housekeeping problems that better-off people do not have to worry about. Transport problems, and the need to buy in small quantities, mean that they may not always be able to buy food as cheaply as other people,[16] though it is difficult to prove, one way or the other, whether the poor do pay more or less for their food. (The evidence suggests that for a given specific item they may pay a few pence more. On the other hand, the premium the better-off pay for 'quality' may be exaggerated: the value for money of stewing steak may be much better than that of rump. An item-by-item comparison of prices is not, therefore, the whole story.) The food problem is made worse if there is not enough money to afford a refrigerator.

A low income may mean the necessity to buy goods that are absolutely cheap (and shoddy) in preference to apparently more expensive (but longer-lasting) items. A very low turnover brings cash-flow problems also. Which is worse, paying more for electricity through a coin meter, or facing a crippling bill every three months? A 20 per cent, even only a 10 per cent, increase in the price of food between benefit reviews or pay rises can make a substantial difference to the standard of living.

It would, no doubt, be possible to recommend a 'sensible' solution to many of these problems. We can suggest that housewives learn to make the most economical use of food, and never give in to the family's wishes for a change, or the occasional luxury. Clothes could be mended for a little longer before they are discarded, and replaced at jumble sales, or even free from the W.R.V.S., if you sacrifice some pride both in obtaining them and in wearing them. If you could save 10p a week for a year, that would provide a little nest-egg of £5 to act as a cushion against weekly variations in expenditure. The list of sensible suggestions could be endless. It is, of course, rather easier to recommend the dominance of sense over sensibility than to put it into perfect practice. Nevertheless, it is clear that *most* poor people are sensible *most* of the time. They have no option. But to suggest therefore that such a budget is reasonable would be to misunderstand the critical importance of the time dimension, as well as the difficulty of maintaining a thick skin in social relationships. Both these problems are well illustrated by the discovery – incomprehensible to the monthly paid middle classes – of the great hardship caused to Supplementary Beneficiaries by the fact that their pay-day came on Monday or Tuesday, not Friday; their pockets were empty at the week-end, just when their neighbours were flush.[17]

The difficulty of long-term budgeting on a level of income intended as an emergency stopgap has already been mentioned. The real difficulty in housekeeping, however sensible one is for most of the time, is in coping with the occasional need for extra expense, which inevitably arises from time to time. An accident or sudden illness cannot be avoided; a wedding and Christmas are expensive items, unless social conventions are simply to be flouted; household goods can break long before they are due to be replaced. Even ignoring these externally imposed emergencies, we should not forget the heavy psychological strain of trying to balance the books week by week for year after year. One or two mistakes one week, and it could take months to recover. In these circumstances it is not surprising if some people are occasionally seduced by the attractive credit facilities in the mail order book into an indiscreet extravagance. Nor is it surprising that the constant strain is so great that the occasional housekeeper gives up the effort to cope altogether. That seems to be more the result of hardship than its cause.

In view of the common criticism that the poor have only to curtail their own extravagance to live within their means, one might be surprised at the lack of extravagance that a comparison of budgets indicates. Table 16 compares small households from the lowest income range with those about national average incomes. The sample sizes are small, so that the precise figures are liable to error.

Table 16   Some weekly expenditure budgets, 1974[18]

| | Single person | | Man and Woman | |
	under £12 per week	£50 p.w. or more	Under £20 per week	£50-£60 per week
Food (excluding meals bought out)	£3.49	£4.73	£6.92	£8.83
Fuel etc.	£1.62	£2.16	£2.32	£2.10
Housing	£2.17	£10.12	£2.80	£6.26
'Other' goods	£0.83	£4.06	£1.46	£3.12
Tobacco	£0.32	£0.93	£1.18	£1.77
Services	£0.95	£8.27	£1.58	£3.32
Clothing etc.	£0.69	£3.52	£1.15	£3.00
Durable household goods	£0.33	£3.86	£0.48	£3.14
Meals bought out	£0.24	£2.13	£0.15	£1.50
Alcoholic drink	£0.27	£2.57	£0.73	£2.41
Transport & vehicles	£0.36	£8.77	£1.09	£6.58
Total	£11.27	£51.12	£19.86	£42.02
(Sample size)	(252)	(125)	(197)	(200)

Food is such an important and inflexible item that the poor people had to spend a far higher proportion of their budget on it than better-off people. Altogether, the poor single person spent over £8 on essentials including food, fuel, housing and 'other' goods (newspapers, soap etc.), leaving only £3.16 for luxuries. The amount spent on these 'luxuries' would buy perhaps a pack of cigarettes, pay the rent on an old TV set and a subscription to a Christmas club, allow for a pair of socks, a payment on a small H.P. instalment, an egg on toast in a café, a pint of mild, and a few bus rides. Not exactly extravagant. Meanwhile, the better-off single person, with two-and-a-half times the expenditure on essentials, was able to spend nine-and-a-half times as much on less necessary items.

There is no need to take a researcher's word for it. Even food, the first basic, is not always available. According to the most recent *National Food Survey*,[19] pensioners as a group seem to be fairly well nourished, although there are certainly exceptions. Low-wage earners, and families with many children are the worst nourished groups on average; these averages must conceal some members of the group who are seriously lacking in certain important foods. Here are some first-hand accounts:[20]

> 'I can't even afford the baby milk, and they go on about the rent arrears.' (*a*) – 'I used to try to save but I can't now. I mean I can't even buy the food I used to.' (*a*) – 'I hadn't got much money and I thought if I went carefully on my food I'd be able to get built up and David (her son) wouldn't go short of anything. At first I had to go without but now it's my fault.' (*c*) – 'When I got down here and there was no gas and electricity, I had next to no money left, and I didn't eat for two days. I was buying meals out for my girl and I was dying for something myself. See, I did tell that to the N.A.B., and they said it was my fault for not managing better. Well, what can you say?' (*a*) – 'I put my mind to it and try to think about something else. And I drink a lot of coffee. It makes me feel sick and I get a bit tired . . . My appetite's gone now. I think with being short of food for so long and not eating much my appetite's just dwindled down.' (*c*) – 'I'd rather the children had the food than I did. It seems to satisfy me more. *They* don't go short, I do.' (*c*) – 'I eat all right, but all I ever eat is bread . . . I can't eat any other sort of things. I can't afford chickens and things like that, and eggs. And if I cut down on bread I get a headache and I get desperately hungry.' (*c*)

Nor are other basics, like heating and lighting, easy to cope with:

> 'The electricity bill's always over £10. I sit in misery sometimes
> at night when I'd like the light on.' (*b*) – 'An unmarried mother
> . . . had had to lie in bed during the day with her clothes on to
> keep warm. A separated wife had had to steal coke at midnight
> from a mill yard.' (*c*) – 'On a Sunday afternoon I'd have the
> electric fire on, but other times I couldn't afford to have the fire
> all the time.' (*b*) – 'In winter I forget I've a dining room, I just
> close the door.' (*c*)

Not surprisingly, poverty is often combined with ill-health, and lack
of means can make ill-health worse:

> 'The hospital says I should go on a diet, but how can I afford it?'
> (*b*) – 'I don't know the last time I tasted a proper piece of
> meat – it's disgusting the price of food.' (*b*) – 'These (spectacles)
> give me a headache . . . but I can't afford.' (*c*) – 'I was told I
> should have hot baths for my arthritis. I have to manage with a
> bucket of hot water. It's just a little bath I need.' (*b*)

More occasional items – clothing and so on – are a special difficulty:

> 'I should like to go and buy something new, but I should never
> be able to wear it.' (*c*) – 'I didn't even have towels or enough
> bed linen and I didn't dare get anything else off the Book, so I
> was going without myself, and her (her daughter's) bed I was
> washing the sheets and putting them back the same night
> because I didn't have any to change them with.' (*a*) – 'I go to
> jumble sales to keep myself clean and tidy.' (*b*) – 'I'm always
> frightened there'll be someone I know (if I go to a jumble sale).'
> (*c*)

Of course there are many little luxuries the rest of us take for granted
which may be impossible for those on Supplementary Benefit:

> 'We had a dog, but it was too expensive. I feel so guilty. The
> children don't mention him, but sometimes they get his photo
> out and then the tears run down their faces.' (*c*) – 'Even the bus
> fares are a worry: its 5p into town and 5p back.' (*a*) – 'If you

stay indoors all the time you're well off – you haven't spent your
money.' (*b*) – 'Christmas day is just like a Sunday. We just have
mince for dinner . . . My bairns never say what they want for
Christmas because they know they can get nothing.' (*a*)

Even so-called free services, such as children's schools, can cost
money:

> 'They used to beg and plead to me for money for cookery
> lessons, but if I hadn't it, if I was really desperate, they
> wouldn't go.' (*c*) – 'I'm worried to death now in case she *does*
> pass the 11-plus. She'll have to have school uniform and she's
> got to have clothes for games, and sports equipment, and I
> don't know where it would come from.' (*c*)

Keeping out of debt is a hard struggle; getting out of it is even harder:

> 'I'm gradually getting worked up to such a pitch because I'm
> robbing Peter to pay Paul, and I'm going short of money to pay
> the Book.' (*a*) – 'If I stopped to write down every little bit that I
> have to pay I'd never get anything. You've just got to stick your
> neck out and then pay for it the week after.' (*c*) – 'I kissed the
> carpet when it was paid for, and said it's mine.' (*b*) – 'There's a
> bloke who comes here every week to lend us money – every-
> body owes him money. We do – that's how we get out of
> trouble. We've been borrowing money to buy the kids' clothes,
> but to borrow £20 you have to pay £28 back.' (*a*) – 'I've always
> got it in the back of my mind to get out of paying for clubs, but
> all the time I get further in, because it's things you've got to
> have.' (*c*)

The risk of debt
As can be seen from some of these illustrations, it is the fear of
getting into debt that is the motive for all the pennypinching that
poverty brings. The motive is clearly a powerful one. Yet it appears
that about half of all S.B. dependants are in debt to formal creditors,
paying about £1 a week of their meagre income to service or repay the
debts.[21] And this is ignoring informal debts with friends or relations,
or *de facto* debts such as postponing payment of rent or electricity.

Perhaps one of the most difficult questions of all in the social security field is that of preventing debt when it is imminent, or the relief of debt once it occurs, whether this was due to unavoidable circumstances, an occasional lapse in good housekeeping, or just bad management.

The Supplementary Benefit Commission does have the power, at its officers' discretion, to make exceptional payments. These can be regular weekly payments to take account of permanent exceptional circumstances – there were 913,000 of these current in 1974, averaging 67p per week,[22] an increase of 89 per cent over 1972. These are mainly associated with sickness or old age, and would tend to cover such things as special diets, extra heating costs and so on. The figures mean that two Supplementary Beneficiaries in seven receive such a payment. Alternatively there can be lump-sum payments for once-occurring exceptional needs, such as replacement of worn-out clothes, bedding or furniture, repairs, funeral expenses and even payment of debts; 830,000 of these one-off payments were made in 1974,[23] about three for every ten regular beneficiaries, if no one received more than one. The average grant was £13.85. Again, such payments are becoming more frequent, the big increase coming between 1971 and 1972.

As a generous society, we would like to be able to give poor people whatever they need, whenever they need it. Unfortunately we feel that this should not degenerate into giving them whatever they want, whenever they want it. This is not purely a matter of the public accounts, even though the current expenditure (based on the figures in the previous paragraph) is to the order of £40 million annually. The real problem of relaxing the rules in granting extra payments (without granting them on demand) is that it would seriously undermine the strength of the motive to budget successfully on the standard weekly income. While it may be that the Commission could and should be more relaxed in particular instances, the consequence of a wholesale relaxation, intended to relieve people of the strains of weekly budgeting, would have the effect of making the strains more intense. Instead of knowing exactly where they stand, beneficiaries would be torn between their instinct to budget on their weekly income, and their hope that if they were to overspend, they might be able to recoup their losses. Yet most people would still be reluctant to go to the Commission for a sub, which, because it depends on a specific request and on the officer's discretion, would still have the odour of charity. And the more grants are given, the more hurtful it would be if a grant were refused.

The system of specific grants designed to reduce the rigours of weekly budgeting on a small income has two essential drawbacks. As long as a specific request to the Commission has to be made, as long as an inquiry into the necessity of the expenditure, and a means test, are the consequences, and as long as there is the possibility of being refused, the grants will appear to be charitable, however much assurance is given that the grants are the right of the citizen. Inevitably this will mean that many people who are genuinely in trouble will not apply for a grant. Moreover, those who do apply for grants undoubtedly feel sore when they are refused, if they think they know of others whose requests have been granted, or if one of their own requests is granted and another is refused. And their limited knowledge of the grant regulations may tempt them into budgeting errors that cannot, in the end, be corrected.

The second consideration is of equity, not between S.B. dependants and the rest of the population (though that cannot be ignored) but among the dependants themselves. The duty is clearly expected of all dependants to live within their means, not only in normal circumstances, but also, if possible, in exceptional circumstances. Most of them are reasonably successful in this, and accept considerable hardship at times in the struggle. Is it fair on them that those who are not successful should be 'bailed out'? What sometimes seems fair to us, considering all the circumstances, does not always seem fair to them, for they feel that their virtue should have some other reward. This problem applies in particular to those claimants who have declared savings to the Commission, and who, of course, are expected to bail themselves out, if necessary.

There is probably no ideal solution to this problem, although a general and substantial increase in S.B. rates would go a long way towards it. The current system of emergency grants does not really meet it. Everyone has his own pet idea as to how social security problems could be solved overnight, which everyone else thinks is ridiculous. But it might help many, though of course not all, beneficiaries, if a system was devised to assist directly with the problem of budgeting for occasional expenditure with a weekly income. Suppose that, as well as the tokens exchangeable for the weekly payment, each beneficiary had a weekly credit to a separate account in the Post Office specifically intended as a savings account.

Would the fact that this distinction had been made, and that a special withdrawal was required, encourage many people to leave the money there (attracting interest) until it was specially needed? A system of credit on the same account, with simple rules governing the level of credit and the programme of repayment, might again help the budgeting problem without perhaps bringing in other problems or the stigma of other forms of debt. A small local pilot scheme along these lines might well indicate a possible solution, even if it did not itself prove workable.

Unfortunately, it does not seem possible to do away with the specific discretionary grant system altogether. There will always be some exceptional expenditures (funeral expenses, for instance) which cannot be coped with otherwise, without causing great hardship; and it also seems that there will always be a handful of people who simply cannot or will not cope with budgeting problems. What else can we do for the Darlington mother who burns her children's clothes when they are finally too dirty to wear? We cannot let the children run naked. But for most people, most of the time, such grants do not really help with the problems of keeping themselves for long periods on an income that is too low to permit any flexibility.

Complexities of the Social Security system

On p. 63 the two prerequisites for adequate living on a low income were said to be a first-class housekeeper and a first-class domestic lawyer. Most of the ensuing discussion has concerned the housekeeper, although the lawyer is needed to make the most of the grants system. But the lawyer's principal function is to understand the regular non-discretionary network of social security benefits, to ensure that:

1 The household's income is as high as possible.
2 As many goods and services as possible are supplied free.
3 Reduced amounts are paid both for goods and services and for other contributions, such as rates.

The number and range of different social security benefits is the subject of much discussion these days. There are reported to be some thirty-four means-tested benefits alone. Just to start with a list of the better-known ones is quite impressive:

Supplementary Benefit
Family Income Supplement
Rent Rebates
Rates Rebates
Prescriptions
Dental Charges
School Meals
School Uniforms
Welfare Milk
Educational Maintenance
University Grants
Legal Aid

Most of those could be listed by anyone who simply reads the newspapers regularly, but the list is the tip of the iceberg; below the surface are benefits that hardly anyone has heard of. Britain is said to be in danger of becoming 'a nation of means tests'.[24]

As well as the wide range of means-tested benefits available for any particular household, there is also a wide range between the particular means tests for each benefit between local authorities. Thus the number of different tests is measured not in dozens but in thousands. This will be of little consequence to our domestic lawyer (unless he wishes to work out where he ought to live!), but it does make for inequities between the residents of neighbouring authorities, apart from the administrative confusion.

Means-tested benefits are not, of course, the only benefits. Others are directed not at people who can prove they have low incomes but at people with particular characteristics who need extra money – invalids, old people are common examples. These types of benefit have been with us for some time, but observers have detected a recent tendency towards more of this sort of payment, as a way of avoiding yet more means tests.[25]

Thirdly, there are innumerable benefits in kind, most of which are given to everybody, or to everybody who needs them – medical treatment, schooling, refuse disposal and so on. But another recent trend, both in popular pressure on the government, and in some action, has been for benefits in kind for selected groups of people. Free bus rides and TV licences for the elderly are a reality in some areas, for instance; free telephones are often suggested. The value of these benefits is difficult to assess. They may be advocated as a sort of hidden increase in the old age pension. But suppose the total value of these benefits was £50 in a year; might not the recipient prefer to have the £1 a week and spend it on buses, telephone and TV if he wanted to? In one sense benefits in kind could be seen as a throwback to the days when paupers were given food, not money.

But the principal concern of our 'domestic lawyer' in the poor household is with means tests. Means-tested benefits are mostly of two sorts: some consist of money payments to people with not enough money (e.g. Supplementary Benefit, Family Income Supplement), but most consist of a reduction or total remission of the cost of goods or services for people who cannot afford them (e.g. school meals, prescriptions). In the latter case the means test brings up two questions. Should people of average or above average means pay for them, and should people of below average means be let off? We can scarcely demand that the poor should not be let off, at least unless some form of compensation is provided elsewhere. Moreover, the system of allowing the poor free medicines, school meals and so on is a way of ensuring that they are not tempted to divert their limited funds away from essential items for their own and their children's physical well-being. This is, of course, rather a paternalistic attitude, but it is almost certainly necessary for the protection of *some* people, especially children, who are unable to influence their parents' expenditure.

The alternative question was whether the non-poor should pay. Take prescription and dental charges, which have been see-sawing on and off in recent years; or hospital treatment charges, which have been threatened. The argument put forward has been that those who can afford to should pay (at least in part) for the benefit they receive. It is, however, difficult to see that they receive a benefit so much as a partial removal of a 'disbenefit'. In what way is a man who has received treatment for a disease better off than a man who never had the disease at all? He is in fact worse off, even if there were no financial differential. Charges for treatment impose an inequity between the sick and the whole; the resolution of inequities between the rich and the poor is a separate problem, for which the taxation and welfare systems are responsible.

There are other cases where it is not so much unfair as unnecessary that the non-poor should contribute directly to the cost of benefits provided by state institutions. In 1973-4 nearly two-thirds of all schoolchildren received official school dinners;[26] 15 per cent of them were provided free, but if take-up had been greater, the proportion might have been as much as 20 per cent. It is probable that the proportion of children taking official dinners is far higher in primary schools than in secondary schools – perhaps 80 per cent. If they were all provided free in primary schools, perhaps the proportion would rise as high as 90 per cent. In a situation where virtually everyone would be able to make use of a benefit, there is no apparent reason why it should not be provided free, funded out of (means-tested) taxation, if this avoids a separate specific means test. (There are also questions concerning the proportion of the national income that passes through taxation, and concerning the relation of direct to indirect taxation; but the sums are probably small enough for a correction to be applied elsewhere, without instituting means tests.)

These means-tested state-supplied benefits form a very small proportion of all the state-supplied benefits in the relevant sectors. And the system is bursting with anomalies. Why are drugs supplied free in hospital, but charged on prescription? Why are meals consumed in hospital free, but not in schools? Why are materials used in English classes and chemistry classes supplied free, but not materials used in domestic science classes? Would it not be easier if things that people *need* were free, while they spent money on things they *want*?

These are arguments that can be applied to some specific means tests, not to others. But there are more fundamental arguments applying to the whole range, and it is the range itself which causes the problem. No one, with the possible exception of one or two very rich and very selfish people, objects to the basic concept of a means test to discover who is rich and who is poor, in order to narrow the differential between them. We have a double-progressive income tax, depending on a means test, which is wholly accepted in principle, if not in detail. It is the practical range of means tests that gives rise to objections, of which there are basically two.

The first objection is that many, probably most, means-tested benefits are not being claimed by all the people who would be entitled to them. This has been argued and demonstrated often enough – according to *The Times*:[27]

About 690,000 Supplementary Pensions not taken up.

About 875,000 Rent Rebates not taken up.

About 1,000,000 Rates Rebates not taken up.

About 200,000 Free School Meals not taken up.

About 25,000 Family Income Supplements not taken up.

It may be that some of those who fail to claim a particular benefit are losing only a few shillings as a result. Nevertheless, the failure rates for benefits vary from the appalling to the fantastic. There is clearly something very wrong with a system of income support that fails to have even the limited effect intended for it. Nor is it reasonable to suggest that if people fail to apply for benefits that is their hard luck; hard luck is precisely the condition that the system is designed to eliminate. Moreover, the system itself is largely responsible for its own failure. There seem to be four reasons why people fail to take up their rightful benefits when these include a means test, although all feed heavily on each other:

1 *Lack of knowledge.* The Child Poverty Action Group publishes[28] a poor-man's (literally) guide to social security benefits, explaining as simply as possible how to claim for 19 different benefits of one sort or another. It tries to explain things simply, and no doubt leaves out most of the detail. It is 80 pages long, and almost incomprehensible, but at least that is better than the total incomprehensibility of most other sources of 'information'.

The problem lies only partly with the sources of information, although an improvement even here would be useful. So many of the leaflets for the use of potential applicants are vague; and even where they begin to get specific, they often say that you *may* be entitled to benefit, rarely that you *are* entitled. Many busy administrators much prefer to deal with definite claims instead of discussing the situation and offering information and advice. Even those who deliberately seek information, therefore, will often not obtain it.

But a more fundamental problem is that the rules themselves are difficult to understand; which is one reason why they are not easily explained. Some benefits depend on the answers to more than a dozen questions, no doubt each with its special list of rules for what counts and what does not. Yet even with F.I.S., which is at first sight one of the simplest systems, more families applied and were turned down in 1974 than applied and were accepted.[29] If over 70,000 families *applied* in ignorance, how many *failed to apply* in ignorance?

The third factor is probably the most important cause of imperfect knowledge – the diversity of benefits. There are so many different benefits that most people probably do not know of the existence of some of them, so that there is no hope of take-up. There are so many different sets of rules that many people, having been rejected on one benefit, wrongly think they do not qualify for others. And different benefits have to be juggled against each other: depending on particular circumstances, it may be better to get a rent rebate from the Town Hall than a Supplementary Benefit from S.B.C., and it is only recently that either body has advised claimants which was better.[30] The C.P.A.G. pamphlet takes three pages to explain how to make the calculation.[31]

2 *Inertia.* In any situation where people have to do something in order to get something, some of them will not bother. This inertial resistance is likely to be high if a large number of separate applications is needed for separate small benefits, if the applicant is not sure of his entitlement, if he is nervous of being rejected, if the application is likely to lead him into repeated haggling or endless delays, if he suffers from the 'respectability' emotions discussed below, if he is naturally shy of authority figures, if he has received brusque treatment in the past, if an expensive bus-ride is involved, or if he has difficulty in getting about. Given this list of possible obstacles, perhaps it is not surprising that so many people think it is not worth while claiming the benefits.

3 and 4 *Self-respect* and *shame.* The distinction here has to be made between feelings of *self-respect*, where personal pride objects to the acceptance of dependence on charity, and *shame*, where it is the fear of what other people will think or say that is of importance. Clearly both are based on the same ideas – we might call them the private and public faces of respectability. The importance of the distinction lies in the fact that camouflaging the existence of benefits from outsiders helps overcome shame but it does not always help, may even exacerbate, the problem of self-respect. It is easy for the outsider to underestimate the strength of these problems, but one has only to listen to the poor and the not-quite-poor discuss their attitudes to each other to realise why they exist. And at least some of the officers responsible for the administration of means tests must carry some of the blame. There is plenty of evidence (at least from the 1960s) that the relation between claimant and claims officer is one of mutual suspicion, not mutual trust; and that officers seek to give the least help, not the most, that they can get away with, often relying on their discretion-ary (and largely unquestionable) powers to do so.[32]

This should not, of course, be taken to imply that mistrust between claimant and officer is universal, still less that it is S.B.C. policy that its officers should take a negative attitude.[33] It seems likely that, partly in response to such criticisms, a much more open relationship has been developing. But there is probably still a gap between the policy of administrators and the practice of some front-line officers, who, after all, still meet some real 'scroungers' and may be rather over-zealous in trying to spot them. In any case the conflicting roles between claimant and officer would seem to make mistrust inevitable – the purpose should be to reduce it as much as possible, but as long as officers have the right and duty to refuse what the claimant regards as a justified request, the claimant may feel aggrieved, and may be deterred from making future claims.

Proposals are often made, and even carried out, to attack each of these problems, but the real solution to lack of knowledge does not lie in publicity campaigns, clearer leaflets, or piecemeal simplification of the rules. The real solution to inertia does not lie in lowering each of the possible barriers. The real solution to the problem of self-respect does not lie in public assurances of the citizen's right to benefits and a more sympathetic treatment of applications. The real solution to shame does not lie either in publicity campaigns or in concealment. All these activities would help but not solve the problems. The only solution, in an ideal world, would lie in shifting the responsibility for benefits from the individual claimant to the authorities responsible for paying the benefit. If the system was designed so that *everyone* automatically received *every* benefit to which he was entitled, then, tautologically, the take-up problem would be solved.

This immediately raises the prospect of 18 million households each filling in the thirty-odd forms, each to be checked by a monstrous army of civil servants! But as immediately it becomes apparent how silly it is to have thirty different forms, all asking roughly the same questions, for as many different benefits. We all of us, or almost all of us, have at least one means test administered by the Inland Revenue; by the apparently simple device of asking a few extra questions, and checking the one form for entitlement to all benefits, there would be not more means tests but less – not more civil servants but fewer. And the scale of the operation would justify the use of a computer (to be checked by hand in case of doubt) to decide most questions, where at present minor benefits administered by small authorities could not do so. The fact that different benefits are granted and paid for by different authorities is, from the point of view of the claimant, a merely administrative complication that could be solved by an administrative reform.

If each of the current types of benefit was included in this system under the current set of rules, this would achieve a great deal, although the computer program would be highly laborious. But an immediate consequence of the attempt to write the program would have to be a rationalisation of the relations between the rules. At the moment rent and H.P. commitments are deducted from gross income for some means tests but not for others. Under the new system these things would either be allowed or not, whatever the benefit. Again, children in the household have different effects on different benefits, a complication that could easily be resolved. Secondly, the existence of several different benefits all working to the same end would seem to require resolution into a single system – at present income tax, F.I.S., rent rebates, rates rebates and so on are all methods of reducing the differential between the poor and the not-so-poor, depending variously on income, housing and children. In theory all these could be combined into a single benefit based on long-term need, provided a flexible system for dealing with immediate or temporary problems could also be developed.

All this is highly ambitious, but major steps towards its achievement have been made. Thus the F.I.S. and S.B. means tests already entitle beneficiaries to free school meals and free prescriptions, free welfare milk, free dental treatment and glasses, and free travel to hospital. And the proposed tax-credit scheme was intended to replace the present tax allowance, F.I.S. and family allowances. If these two reforms had been combined, we would have had one means test where we had eight before.

Non-take-up of benefits gives rise to inequities between those who claim and those who do not. But thinking of the possibility of merging benefits makes clear the second main problem caused by the diversity of benefits, which raises different inequities, and also practical questions. This concerns 'marginal rates of taxation/benefit'.

Means-tested benefits are of three different types. The first (e.g. free school meals) depends on an income 'threshold': if your assessed income is above a certain limit, you get no benefit; if below, you get the benefit. The second may be called 'guarantee' benefits (e.g. Supplementary Benefit) in which every pound by which your assessed income falls below a certain amount is automatically made up. Thirdly, there are scale benefits, whereby every pound below a certain level attracts a proportion, less than a pound, of benefit. Thus for F.I.S. it is 50p in the pound, for rate rebates it is 6p or 8p in the £, and for rent rebates it is either 17p or 25p in the £; income tax (where people pay it) is a negative benefit of 35p in the pound.

Some benefits are incompatible – for instance, you cannot claim both S.B. and F.I.S. Others may be self-cancelling, in that benefits obtained in one area are removed from the other. But over the whole range the benefits are usually independent, so that, depending on particular circumstances, it is possible to be eligible for several. It is easy to see (simply by adding together some of the scale rates given above) that cases will often arise where for every pound you lose, you will get a pound or even more back. Conversely, for every pound you gain in wages, you lose more than a pound in benefit. Plenty of theoretical examples have been worked out to demonstrate this. A similar effect is apparent as your income crosses a 'threshold', when you may lose a benefit more valuable than the increased wage.

For the people with the very lowest original incomes, particularly if they have children, this is fine, although even so they are not exactly rolling in luxury. On the other hand, effective marginal rates of over 100 per cent (or even rates above 50 per cent) create a problem with three aspects.

1 *Incentives.* High marginal rates mean that those who work harder for higher wages get little, nothing, or even less than nothing in return. This is bound to discourage people from working harder, even occasionally from working at all. The system therefore discourages a full contribution to the work effort and the economy. Much is said but almost nothing is known about the disincentive effect for people with low earnings (or, for that matter, for the very rich, who also have high marginal tax rates). The effect would be diminished to the extent that people have little opportunity for increasing their own earnings except where voluntary overtime, promotion, or job change are available; to the extent that promotion and job change (and even overtime) may be attractive for non-monetary reasons; to the extent that people find it difficult to calculate their effective marginal rate (one advantage of the diversity of benefits!); to the extent that people seek independence of state benefits for its own sake; or to the extent that people are

able to conceal their additional earnings (by working 'foreigners', for instance).

2 *The poverty trap.* While disincentives may deter people from seeking to increase their earnings, the 'poverty trap' affects those who have increased their earnings. In this situation people who obtain promotion or a pay rise find themselves worse off than they were before. The difficulty of calculating your marginal rate makes the trap more of a painful surprise than it would otherwise be. In practice the poverty trap is probably less sharp than it is in theory, because of time lags in assessments, non-take-up, and so on. Theoretical examples of how it might work abound, but families who have suffered a fall in income following a pay rise are rather harder to find. Nevertheless, the poverty trap is important as an anomaly that has been built into the present system.

3 *Equity.* While disincentives and the poverty trap affect particular people as their situation changes, there is also the question of equity between different people. If a man with higher wages has a lower net income than a man (with the same commitments) with lower wages, the whole system of differential wages is thrown into question.

This problem has clearly arisen as a result of the diversity of benefits developed *ad hoc* to meet various situations. It cannot possibly be resolved without a total review of the benefit system, such as would result from the sort of reform discussed earlier. Then it would be possible to discuss what sorts of marginal rates did and should apply to various kinds of people.

Not that the answer would follow easily from that analysis, for we seem very keen to have our cake as well as eating it. If we want to reduce the distinction between the poor and the average, high marginal rates of taxation or benefit are inevitable somewhere. One alternative is to have very high marginal rates for poor people, resulting in a low differential between poor and average – this is the selectivist policy currently pursued. The other alternative is to have universal benefits, with the extra costs coming out of universal taxation – with the result that marginal tax rates go up for the rest of society, and the differential between the poor and the average is less effectively closed.

These alternatives can be simply illustrated by assuming society to consist of seven people with wages of £10, £20, £30, £40, £50, £60, and

£70 respectively. The selective policy brings the income of the lowest paid up to, say £20, while the £10 cost is paid by the over £20 earners in proportion to the excess of their incomes over £20.

Table 17 Selective policy

Original income	Net income	Marginal rate (per cent)	Percentage of Median net income
£10	£20.00	100/6⅔	52
£20	£20.00	6⅔	52
£30	£29.33	6⅔	76
£40	£38.67	6⅔	100
£50	£48.00	6⅔	124
£60	£57.33	6⅔	148
£70	£66.67		172

The universalist policy gives, say, £10 to each person, the £70 paid for by the £20-and-over earners in proportion to the excess of their original incomes over £20.

Table 18 Universalist policy

Original income	Net income	Marginal rate (per cent)	Percentage of Median net income
£10	£20.00	Zero	49
£20	£30.00	Zero/46	74
£30	£35.33	46	87
£40	£40.67	46	100
£50	£46.00	46	113
£60	£51.33	46	126
£70	£56.67	46	139

Under the first system the very poorest man has gained substantially on his immediate neighbours, but has a high marginal rate. Under the second, the second and third man get the greatest relative advantage; the poorest two have a very low tax rate, but the rest of society has a high rate (on top of previously existing taxation), with possible disincentive effects.

No doubt some acceptable compromise can be found. But it cannot be found under present circumstances, when we do not know which people experience which marginal rates, either *de jure* (assuming full take-up of benefit) or *de facto* (given non-take-up). It is the sort of information that a complex, but feasible, survey would provide. Such a survey would also provide a valuable model on which to try out the effects of alternative proposals for reform.

It is appreciated that reforms of the kind discussed cannot be expected to be achieved tomorrow afternoon. British society has usually preferred 'creeping incrementalism' to Alexandrine ruthlessness. Hence the tangle of knots we now face. But every now and then the need to rationalise past progress becomes apparent. What we need is a new Beveridge.

NOTES

1 Dept. of Health and Social Security, *Social Security Statistics, 1974*, H.M.S.O. Further references to this source in this chapter will be noted as *S.S.S. '74*
2 *S.S.S. '74*
3 *S.S.S. '74*
4 Persons over pensionable age, divided by total population – 1971 census.
5 *S.S.S. '74*
6 Based on figures in *The Times*, 14 October 1975.
7 *S.S.S. '74*
8 *S.S.S. '74*
9 A. Lynes, 'Policy on Social Security', in M. Young (ed.), *Poverty Report 1974*, Maurice Temple Smith, 1974.
10 B. Abel-Smith and P. Townsend, *The Poor and the Poorest*, Bell, 1965.
11 *S.S.S. '74*
12 See C. Trinder, 'People Not at Work', in M. Young (ed.), *Poverty Report 1975*, Maurice Temple Smith, 1975.
13 *S.S.S. '74*
14 See, e.g., W. W. Daniel, *A National Survey of the Unemployed*, PEP Broadsheet No. 546, 1974.
15 *1971 Census*, Summary Tables (1 per cent sample).
16 See D. Piachaud, *Do the Poor Pay More?*, Child Poverty Action Group, 1974.
17 D. Marsden, *Mothers Alone*, Penguin, 1969.
18 Dept. of Employment, *Family Expenditure Survey 1974*, H.M.S.O., 1975.
19 O.P.C.S., *Household Food Consumption and Expenditure 1973*, H.M.S.O., 1975. See also report in *New Society*, 29 May 1975.
20 Quotations marked (*a*) are taken from interviews carried out for PEP as part of the present study. Quotations marked (*b*) are taken

from L. Syson and M. Young, *op. cit.* Quotations marked (*c*) are taken from D. Marsden, *op. cit.*

21 Dept. of Health and Social Security, *Families Receiving Supplementary Benefit*, H.M.S.O., 1972.
22 *S.S.S. '74*
23 *S.S.S. '74*
24 Quoted (without reference) in R. Holman, *Socially Deprived Families in Britain*, 1973 Supplement, Bedford Square Press.
25 A. Lynes, 'Policy on Social Security', *op. cit.*
26 Dept. of Education and Science, *Statistics of Education*, Vol. V.
27 *The Times*, 14 October 1975.
28 C.P.A.G., *National Welfare Benefits Handbook*, Poverty Pamphlet 13, fifth edition, November 1975
29 *S.S.S. '74*
30 See L. Syson and M. Young, 'The Camden Survey', *op. cit.*
31 C.P.A.G., *National Welfare Benefits Handbook, op. cit.*
32 See especially D. Marsden, *op. cit.*, and S. Sinfield: 'Poor and Out of Work in Shields', in P. Townsend (ed.), *The Concept of Poverty*, Heinemann Educational Books, 1970.
33 See O. Stevenson, *Claimant or Client*, Allen & Unwin, 1973.

3 Housing

Housing is so important, both physically and socially, that the lack of reasonable accommodation can become a dominant problem in a family's fortunes. Housing is a field where the social goals can be fairly clearly stated; yet the exigent growth of demand and the heavy restraints on supply make the achievement of those goals extraordinarily difficult.

Housing problems and progress

There are several standard indicators of the adequacy or inadequacy of housing. The situation in the early 1970s was as shown in Table 19.

Table 19 Measures of inadequate housing, 1971[1]

	per cent
(a) Dwellings considered unfit	7
(b) Households living at a density of	
more than 1.0 person per room	6
more than 1.5 persons per room	1
(c) Households lacking one bedroom	6
two bedrooms	1
(d) Households *sharing* a bath/shower	3
lacking a bath/shower	9
sharing an inside W.C.	3
with the sole use of an	
outside W.C.	10
sharing an *outside* W.C.	1
with *no* W.C. *at all*	1

There is clearly a good deal of overlap between these figures, in that, for instance, many of the unfit houses will have no bath or inside W.C., and some may be overcrowded in addition. The overlap reduces the number of households affected below the figure one

84

would reach simply by adding the separate items together, but, of course, makes the situation of the worst-off households even more unfortunate. Even so, perhaps as many as one household in five or six has housing in some respect below the minimum standards that have been accepted for some years; perhaps 3 million households come into this category.

Not all these households are living in abject misery. Young single people will often accept housing in which they share the bathroom with one or two others, in preference to paying a higher rent for a bathroom of their own. They are more robust than children or old people, and the total pressure of persons on the facilities may not be excessive. Similarly, a W.C. immediately outside the kitchen door of an otherwise satisfactory home is not a major problem, by comparison with the detached privies some people have to contend with.

There nevertheless remains a core of households whose accommodation is shocking. Some are so crowded that there are not even enough beds, let alone enough rooms, to ensure privacy or even sufficient sleep. There are homes where every drop of hot water has to be heated on the stove; where a bath means a flannel and a bucket, or a trip to public amenities; and where a visit to the toilet necessitates a trek through cold and rain to an unlit privy whose door has been damaged by vandals. In some houses the walls are crumbling, dirty and mouldy with damp. There are few homes as bad as this, but there are far too many; and there are too many homes not so bad as this, which are unacceptable by comparison with the majority, but which have to be accepted for lack of an alternative.

Housing poverty is visible poverty. You can see it just by walking through the areas where it is concentrated. You can begin to imagine what it is like to live in poor housing just by walking through the door, and you can communicate a sense of it by taking photographs.

It is also visible to those who live in poor housing. There is no escape from the fact of poor housing, and the householders know that their poverty is visible to others, bringing pity, stigmatisation and shame. That in itself is perhaps as demoralising as the inconvenience, the discomfort, and the bronchitis. Housing problems are perhaps the most serious form of deprivation.

Now the good news. Considering the scale of the problem, and the financial cost and the scarcity of land, the situation seems to be improving rapidly (Table 20).

Table 20 Changes in Inadequate Housing[2]

	1964 percent	1966 percent	1967 percent	1971 percent
(a) Unfit dwellings			12	7
(b) Households lacking bedrooms	9			6
(c) Households with more people than rooms		6.5		4.8
(d) Households lacking a bath/shower			15	9
(e) Households without sole use of a W.C.			7.8	4.5

These improvements are not unimpressive, and if they have not benefited those who have been left behind, we can at least begin to see the possibility that these particular types of housing problem will be eliminated. On the other hand, we should not forget that deprivation, as we now understand it, is not absolute but relative. It is not so very long ago that many homes we now consider inadequate were considered quite reasonable; new houses were constructed with outside W.C.s and even without baths. The trend in acceptability can most easily be seen in the case of density of occupation – as recently as the 1950s the level of unacceptability was over two persons per room; it is now officially over one and half persons per room, and unofficially over one person per room, as a result of a continuing downward trend in average densities. Similarly, we will soon be rejecting the 'bedroom standard' devised in 1960, on the grounds that most families are not doubling up teenage children, even of the same sex, and in any case prefer a spare room.

In the case of the other indicators, where it appears that the household is either up to standard or not, it is not so easy to see how a general improvement could change the standards of adequacy. Can the criteria for 'fitness' change? Or do the experts who assess fitness automatically raise their standards in line with modern technical developments? It is possible to guess at some of the future standards: a second (downstairs) W.C. for families with children; full central heating as mandatory in the future as electric power points are now; electric waste-disposal units as necessary as main drainage. None of these possibilities seem very far-fetched in the long term, given the changes in standards that have taken place, and given the standards now current in some middle-class homes, or in homes in some other countries. In spite of the general improvement towards our current standards, there will probably never come a time when those concerned with housing problems can shake each other by the hand and congratulate themselves on a job well done.

These future possibilities raise important questions for current policy. The houses and flats that are now being pulled down, or renovated, are inadequate either because they have deteriorated below the standard to which they were designed, or because they were designed to a standard below what we now consider acceptable. Given a minimum quality of construction and materials, deterioration need not be such a problem, provided owners or occupiers have sufficient incentive for continuous maintenance and repairs–it is generally lax maintenance that has resulted in homes becoming unfit.[3] On the other hand, if standards continue to rise, the homes we are building *en masse* today may be as unsuitable in only fifty years' time as are so many of those built only fifty years ago. Part of this built-in obsolescence is to do with architectural style–the current maximisation of window space and the minimisation of walls and corridors in the living area could not necessarily have been foreseen between the wars, and there is no reason to believe that we can foresee future styles. But the other part of obsolescence is concerned with standard facilities, where reasonable guesses may be possible. Should we be building in these future facilities now, to prevent the perpetuation of inadequate housing? Or designing homes so that they can easily be improved? Or should we lower our standards of home construction, on the admission that it is not worth building a hundred-year house which will be obsolete in fifty years?

Construction and improvement

Construction activity is necessary for two reasons: the elimination of substandard housing, and the provision of an increased total stock. Taking the elimination of substandard housing first, there are two modes of operation.

One is the total demolition of unfit homes, making way for new houses and flats in their place. Until recently up to 90,000 dwellings were being demolished annually in Great Britain–mostly, but not all, unfit. The numbers fell abruptly to only 53,000 in 1974 but are again increasing.[4] Most of this work has been in general slum clearance schemes, where whole areas have been knocked down to be replaced. Since the number of unfit homes has been declining, it is clear that unfit homes have been demolished more quickly than previously fit homes have deteriorated below the standards required. In terms of the statistics the action is being successful, but in terms of people it is evident that some local authorities have not been much more sensitive than the bulldozers they employ, with the result that the people have not benefited as much as they ought from redevelopment.

It was partly in order to avoid these social problems caused by wholesale slum clearance that policy turned to financial support for improvement of substandard properties, as an alternative to demolition and replacement. The new policy was also logical, as the worst slums were already going, so that attention could be turned to homes that were not wholly inadequate, and could be made adequate for a comparatively modest price. The rise of improvement grants was spectacular: there were 114,000 'discretionary' grants approved in the summer quarter of 1973 alone, compared with less than 59,000 in the whole of 1968.[5] If we add in the 'standard' grants, improvements were running at a rate of half a million homes a year at that peak in 1973. Since then there has been a substantial drop in the number of improvement grants approved – partly as a result of a reduction of the rate of grant in special areas; partly because of more stringent conditions; but probably mainly as a result of lack of cash among councils and private owners, stemming from the changing economic climate.

At the peak, however, they were impressive figures, even if we admit that not all the homes affected were very seriously deficient before improvement, or that not all are completely adequate even after improvement. In Westminster, for instance, over half the dwellings improved between 1967 and 1972 still had basic facilities less than required for the number of households occupying them.[6] But sharing is a special problem for central London. Nevertheless, a number of drawbacks have already appeared.

Owner-occupiers of substandard property can often not afford to pay their half of the improvement bill, necessary before they can attract the other half in a grant. Some small private landlords will be in the same position. Larger private landlords have no motive for making the necessary investment unless they see the prospect of a return in the form of increased rent. In some special areas these financial disincentives have been tackled by offers of 60 per cent, 75 per cent or even (in cases of hardship) 90 per cent of the cost in grant. On the other hand, some tenants or owner-occupiers of substandard properties may be sufficiently accustomed to their situation to prefer it to the cost, inconvenience and loss of living space arising from the installation of, for instance, a bathroom. In general it may be that the family living in an improved home may have more in common with families living in already adequate homes than with those still living in poor housing.[7] It can therefore be alleged that improvement policy is being effective in gradually extending good housing down the social scale, only to the exclusion of the housing poor. The latter may be even worse off, caught in an ever-tightening squeeze. At worst, grants could simply be giving financial aid to people who would have lived in decent housing anyway.

The other aspect of construction work is to make net additions to the stock of homes, whether locally to absorb local migration, nationally to accommodate the increasing population, or, in either case, to release any frustrated demand. Over the past decade or so several hundred thousand dwellings were completed every year, rising fairly steadily from just over 300,000 in 1961 to over 400,000 in 1967 and 1968, and falling fairly steadily since to 304,000 in 1972.[8] For most of that period the upward and then downward trends were mainly the responsibility of the public sector: while private sector completions fluctuated around the 200,000 mark, the public sector rose from 100,000 to 200,000 and then started falling back again. But, in 1973 and 1974, it was the private sector that slumped, pulling the total completions down below 300,000 in 1974, in spite of a strengthening of public-sector activity. Both sectors now appear to be slowly increasing, and have regained the 300,000 mark.

From these figures we need to subtract the annual number of demolitions, to arrive at an estimate of net increase, so that the true addition is more in the region of 100,000 to 200,000 every year. Here we are reminded of a major problem for the public sector. Those councils with the worst housing problems have virtually run out of fresh land on which to build (apart from occasional windfalls from closures of railway yards, docks etc.) and can build new homes only by demolishing old ones, either their own out-of-date estates or compulsorily purchased slums from private ownership. It is therefore virtually impossible to make a sizeable net increase in the stock of dwellings in these areas without building at unacceptable levels of crowding–particularly since tower blocks have been ruled out on social grounds.

It is extremely difficult to evaluate these home construction figures on the basis of whether it is 'enough', since the required quantity depends on whether the stock was sufficient to begin with, on the distinction between gross and net increases, on the distinction between new buildings and refurbishment of old buildings, on the growth of population, on changes in the structure of the population, and on the intimate link between supply and demand. One writer lays down as rule of thumb that a country needs to produce roughly ten homes per year per 1,000 population,[9] which would mean over 500,000 for the United Kingdom, a figure we can reach only if we add a substantial proportion of the improvements to our new construction figures. On the other hand, the rule of thumb begs so many questions about a country's social structure and social history as to be unreliable if applied to any one particular country.

Between 1961 and 1971 this country's population increased by about 5 per cent; the *adult* population by only 4 per cent, perhaps a better indication in the apparent need for extra homes. But the number of *households* increased by as much as 12 per cent.[10] Meanwhile, the stock of dwellings seems to have increased by 15 per cent.[11] In fact, over the country as a whole (though not necessarily in each part of it), it is now possible to say that there are more dwellings than there are households.

These figures certainly seem to indicate that considerable progress has been made in the size of the housing stock in relation to needs in recent years. Judged solely on the relative numbers of dwellings and households enumerated, they might even be taken as a justification for the falling production since 1967-8, although not for a lengthy continuation of that trend. And yet scarcity of housing is still acute, as witnessed by the statistics on homelessness and the catastrophic increases in the prices of owner-occupied homes that occurred in 1972 and 1973.

At first sight the nature of demand for housing seems fairly simple: given a certain number of households, a certain number of homes will be required for them. Unfortunately, housing is so vital that it is an indispensable part of new household formation; restriction in the supply of housing is bound to restrict the *apparent* demand for it to the extent that apparent demand (the number of households in existence) always appears to be filled. The hidden part of the real demand manifests itself only when the housing is provided to permit households to form freely. The fact that the *population of households* has been increasing more rapidly than the *population of persons* is at least partly explained by the fact that more housing has been provided as the *stock of dwellings* has increased.

The supply of houses may be at least as powerful a determinant of household structure as are demographic, economic and other social factors. And in turn, any demographic, economic or other social factors that do tend towards more and smaller households will strengthen the hidden demand for housing. The trouble is that the population is so large, and the building industry so small in relation to it, that comparatively slight forces in the one can overwhelm the other. About 1.4 per cent of all households contain two or more families;[12] 250,000 houses would be needed to solve this problem. If the average couple wish to get married one year earlier than at present, a permanent increase in the housing stock of over 350,000 would be required. No one has any reliable knowledge of the numbers of current households that would fragment if the housing market eased – couples living with the girl's parents, old people unable to locate a suitable flat near their children, marriages held together only by the need for shelter, young couples postponing marriage, and so on – but if it was a mere 5 per cent of the household population, as some data suggest, then we still lack up to a million homes, which would need to be provided over and above satisfying other demographic demands. The fact that the population of households has expanded with the supply of housing is evidence that there has been this hidden demand of households 'waiting to come out of the woodwork'; but there is little evidence that it has yet been satisfied.

Unfortunately, simply increasing the total supply of housing will not always solve these problems. The experience of some housing managers in areas where supply exceeds demand suggests it becomes extremely difficult to find tenants for the less popular estates, which rapidly decay as a result. Quality must therefore be improved at the same time as quantity.

Meanwhile, one consequence of the easing of the supply of housing and of the trend towards smaller households has been a reduction in the amount of overcrowding, as measured by the density of persons per room. Table 21 indicates that the trend is as much explained by smaller households occupying the same-sized homes, as by larger homes accommodating the same-sized households.

Table 21 Trends in average density of occupation, 1931–71[13]

	1931	1951	1961	1966	1971
Persons per household	3.75	3.21	3.06	2.99	2.91
Rooms per household	4.37	4.22	4.50	4.60	4.62
Persons per room	0.86	0.76	0.68	0.65	0.63

Tenure and the homeless

All the current changes mentioned so far, whatever riders may be added, seem to indicate a trend, often fairly impressive, towards a better physical stock of homes for people to live in. Similarly, an ever-increasing proportion of the population is obtaining its housing on the best possible terms, through owner-occupation; and the proportion unable to buy who have an acceptable next best–council tenancy–is also increasing, though more slowly. On the whole the housing situation seems to be improving. But housing is a field where constant care needs to be taken to ensure that statistics intended for use as indicators of trends should not be allowed to obscure the picture of the minorities not directly affected by the trend. Yet the statistics most directly relevant to housing stress for the minority show not an improvement, but a steady deterioration. At the beginning of the 1960s considerable concern was expressed as the number of homeless families in welfare accommodation in London passed the 1,000 mark.[14] The figure is now over 3,000–over 4,000 if we include those in bed-and-breakfast accommodation under council auspices. Nor, as was the case in the 1950s, are the figures susceptible to up-and-down fluctuations–they are continuously rising (Table 22).

Table 22   Cases of Homelessness[15]

	1969	1970	1971	1972	1973
Greater London	3,368	3,666	3,918	5,933	7,829
Elsewhere in England and Wales	—	—	3,351	3,745	5,106

This increase in the number of families temporarily accommodated cannot be explained in terms of increased supply of emergency accommodation–there were about three applications for each admission throughout this period in London. In spite of the unreliability of the statistics, and no matter what theories are put forward about how and why people declare themselves homeless, it is clear that the general numerical improvement in the housing stock is being accompanied by increasing particular problems, which in some cases are reaching a crisis.[16]

The numbers of homeless are not large in relation to the total population. But bearing in mind those whose applications are turned down, and those whose situation is equally desperate until another emergency solution is found; and bearing in mind the nature of the distress imposed, it is clear that for many people the housing situation is getting not better, but worse. It is difficult to avoid the conclusion that this minority is not just being left out of the general improvement; is being more deprived, not only relative to the improved situation for others; but is being made positively worse off by the processes at work in the housing market.

In view of the many trends both in housing and in other aspects of society that coincide with the increase in homelessness, it is difficult to single out one to bear the responsibility. But clearly much of the explanation will lie in that sector of the housing market where the worst conditions exist, which is also the sector to which the potentially homeless would turn as a last-resort-but-one.

In 1973 14 per cent of all households rented their accommodation from private landlords – 11 per cent unfurnished, 3 per cent furnished.[17] Some of these homes are perfectly satisfactory, and others, in the furnished sector, are sufficient for young people staying a short time. On the other hand, the private sector has far more than its appropriate share of the nation's housing problems:[18]

52 per cent of the unfit dwellings (E. & W.) are privately rented (excluding those of the 15 per cent of unfit dwellings that were vacant or closed, which would have been privately rented had there been a tenant).
34 per cent of the homes built before 1919 are privately rented.
62 per cent of households *sharing* a bath or shower rent privately, mostly furnished.
52 per cent of households with *no* bath or shower *at all* rent privately, almost all of them unfurnished.
71 per cent of households *sharing* a W.C. rent privately.
49 per cent of households with an outdoor W.C. rent privately, mainly unfurnished.
56 per cent of households with *no* W.C. *at all* rent privately, almost all unfurnished.

As a general rule, therefore, we can say that bad housing tends to be privately rented housing. Perhaps it is possible to generalise further that private unfurnished homes are likely to be absolutely bad through unfitness or total lack of vital amenities, while furnished homes have problems specifically related to the form of tenure: sharing of basic amenities between households, as well as (at least until recently) lack of long-term security.

The people living in privately rented accommodation are principally those without dependants. In the unfurnished sector they are mainly elderly – 49 per cent of all unfurnished tenancies are held by single people aged 60 or more, or by a pair of adults, one or both of whom is aged 60 or over. Conversely, the furnished sector is populated by young adults: 65 per cent of the households are single adults under 60 or a pair of adults both under 60; 57 per cent of heads of household are under 30.[19]

There are, of course, particular reasons for particular types of people living in privately rented accommodation. The elderly moved into their homes many years ago, when private tenure was much more common than it is now, and when, for instance, outside W.C.s were considered much less unacceptable. Simply by reason of their own age, they tend, on average, to live in older property, which, because neither they nor their landlord can (or will) afford to maintain it properly, tends to become unfit around them. They cannot move to better private accommodation because they would lose the protection from exorbitant rent increases provided by their security of tenure. They do not want to move anyway for emotional reasons, and the council therefore can do little for them. The problem would seem to be that the members of each generation tend to equip themselves with housing during their working lives. By the time they reach old age, the property will be ageing itself, and in need of repair; their financial circumstances will prevent either repairs or a move; and, in any case, as standards of acceptability improve, their homes will have become relatively unacceptable. There is little that can obviously be done for them, although perhaps the council could impose itself as an intermediate landlord between tenant and owner, in order to protect the elderly from pressure, and to carry out such improvements and repairs as are possible without disruption. In this case the answer may be a temporary municipalisation of the tenancy rather than a permanent municipalisation of the property.

For young unattached people in furnished accommodation the situation is quite different. Here the reasons are associated with their age and household structure, rather than the generation they were born into. There is a positive demand for furnished rooms for short terms, among young people, particularly the unmarried, who do not yet wish for the commitment of an owner-occupied home, and are quite prepared to accept some lowering of standards if this is for a short period, and if it saves rent compared with a better-provided flat.

The private sector is therefore highly polarised, at one end for acceptable reasons, at the other end for apparently unavoidable reasons. On the other hand, the polarisation should not be allowed to obscure the situation for those private tenants who are neither young and footloose, nor old and static. A minority of the households in the minority tenures are in neither category, but the minority is not that small in terms of numbers.

Table 23 Approximate number of certain types of household in the private sector[20]

	Unfurnished	Furnished
Small families	499,000	132,000
Large families	174,000	23,000
Large adult households*	412,000	60,000

*Some large adult households will be loose confederations of students or other young people, and may therefore come in the young and footloose category. This 'clubbing' of young people may make the market even tighter for families.

These perfectly ordinary households living in private sector housing add up to 1,300,000 – over 200,000 in furnished accommodation. On the other hand, the statistics on homelessness (over 30,000 applications in England and Wales in 1973, over 12,000 families admitted) begin to look a good deal less insignificant in this context.

There are, then, many families still living under a tenure that not only has drawbacks in itself – problems connected with security, and with decoration and repairs – but is also likely to include serious housing problems connected with the physical structure and amenities. Nor are these problems coincidental. It is the landlord's inability (or unwillingness) to maintain or improve his property that causes privately rented homes of a given age to be more likely to be unfit or with inadequate facilities than council homes or owner-occupied homes of the same age.

An instinctive reaction to the problems of private tenure may therefore be to propose the elimination of the private rental sector (or, if we think landlords are wicked, put 'an end to the private landlord'). Of course, this is a process that seems to be well on its way. At the beginning of this century owner-occupation was the privilege of a few, and council housing had not been invented. Virtually everyone rented his home either from a private landlord or from his employer. Fig. 2 shows how we have already reached the situation where over half our homes are owner-occupied, over a quarter are council tenancies and less than one-fifth are private tenancies, including 5 per cent 'others' (mostly connected with

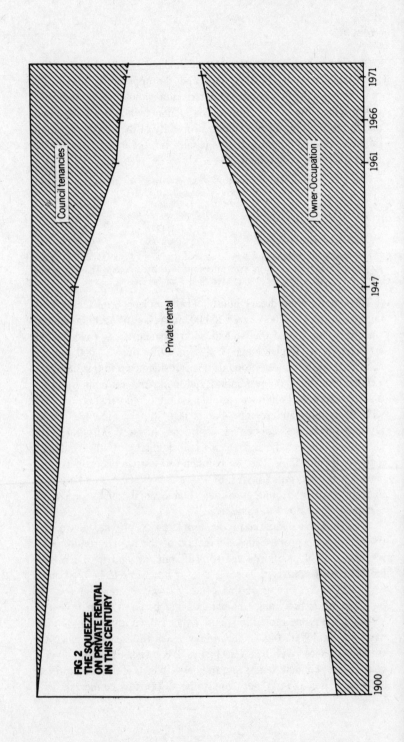

FIG 2
THE SQUEEZE
ON PRIVATE RENTAL
IN THIS CENTURY

Council tenancies

Owner-Occupation

Private rental

1900   1947   1961   1966   1971

employment).[21] And the processes that have brought about this situation are still at work; if we were to extrapolate the 1960s trend through the 1970s, we would reach two-thirds owner-occupied, one-third council tenancies and no private tenancies around 1983. However, this is far too simple an assumption to qualify in any way as a 'prediction'.

From many points of view these trends seem to be entirely desirable. Owner-occupation is undoubtedly the best form of tenure in providing a family with stability, freedom to make their house into a home of their own, freedom to move when and where they will, protection against inflation, and no costs to incur in old age, once the mortgage is paid off. In spite of the high initial costs (currently enormous for those trying to buy for the first time after the 1972-3 burst of house price increases and interest rates) and in spite of the unnecessarily high incidental costs of moving from one owner-occupied house to another, the spread of owner-occupation seems to be a 'good thing'. Similarly, for those who cannot afford a home of their own, a council tenancy is usually next best, preferable to a private tenancy because of the moral commitment of the council 'landlord' to satisfactory housing, reasonable rents, and fair play, a moral commitment that most councils keep to most of the time. There are, of course, substantial improvements that could be made in council housing as a tenure, especially in choice between properties and in freedom to move. Nevertheless, for those with little economic power, the rise of council housing should, in itself, also be considered a 'good thing'.

On the other hand, as we look towards the point when council housing and owner-occupation have finally squeezed out private rental, we ought perhaps to start to worry about the social consequences. In the first half of the century a basically one-tenure society was replaced by a three-tenure society; in the second half we shall end up with a two-tenure society. While both of the surviving tenures are undoubtedly better than the obsolete one, the division between two radically different and unequal tenures may well serve to ossify a division into two societies. Secondly, when private tenure ceases to provide food for the growth of the two currently dominant tenures, they are likely to start to look to each other for nourishment. There does not seem to be much doubt that owner-occupation will succeed in eating away at council tenancies; while this may be desirable for the new owner-occupiers, the tendency would then be for council tenants to be isolated again into the deprived class from which council housing was originally intended to rescue them.

This discussion has concentrated on the growth of owner-occupation and council tenancies, and has so far treated the decline of the private rental sector simply as the negative side of this tendency. Given that private rental is the third-best tenure, which for most people it undoubtedly is, its decline seems desirable. But, again given its undesirability, it is clear that people live in privately rented homes not just because such homes exist, but also because homes are not available for them on better terms. No better alternative exists, otherwise they would take it. For those on low pay, or with large families, or with fluctuating employment, there is no question of owner-occupation; the choice would therefore be between council housing and private rental.

In some parts of the country there is not a serious shortage of council housing, so that couples can obtain decent accommodation after at most a short wait. But elsewhere, particularly in the big cities, the shortage of council housing is acute; or, in effect, there is no council housing 'on the market' at all. All the council homes are already full, often of middle-aged people who either obtained them during council housing's main period of growth, or who waited a long time to get to the head of the queue. (In Westminster, for instance, the average age of council tenants moving in in the past five years is over 50.)[22] Council housing is available only for those who have lived in the area for a very long time; or, increasingly, who lived in old housing that was demolished to make way for redevelopment; or, unfairly, whose homelessness was so desperate that they were forced to jump the queue. In order to get a council home a family must either subject itself to a lengthy purgatory in barely adequate private housing, or gamble on an even worse period in acutely bad housing in the hope of jumping the queue. In this situation privately rented housing is the only alternative. Where else can they go? And with the decline of the private sector, that alternative becomes less and less available.

> . . . the rabbits in the cornfield syndrome – as the harvester cuts its way round the periphery of the field towards the ever diminishing standing corn in the centre, the strongest rabbits make a dash from the centre across the cut corn to the field hedges. The rest are cut to pieces when the harvester reaches the centre.[23]

Of course, if 1,000 privately rented homes are demolished and replaced by 1,000 council homes, the net effect on the total housing stock is nil. There may even be some slight relaxation in the council sector. Unfortunately, council housing is inflexible; when it replaces private housing, it destroys what little flexibility there was in the market. The housing problems of those who are rehoused by the council are solved, but those who would later have obtained housing in the old private homes have to turn elsewhere. As the private sector is boiled away, the housing poor are ever more concentrated within it; the problems of the private sector become more acute; the pressure for its elimination becomes greater. The circle may be at least as vicious as the landlords!

So, until council housing can flexibly meet the demand for immediate housing for those who need it, or until some new alternative (such as housing associations) can build up its strength in numbers, the decline of the third-best alternative will mean that people will increasingly turn to the fourth-best – temporary accommodation for the homeless. This can be seen most clearly in London, where the greater demand for a flexible housing market has meant the longer preservation of the private sector (still $26\frac{1}{2}$ per cent privately rented in 1971/2, against 14 per cent in the whole of Great Britain), [24] and where, conversely, its rapid decline has most effect. London, with 14 per cent of the households in England and Wales, has over half the homeless. Moreover they stay, on average, far longer in temporary accommodation than elsewhere, and have, in the end, through a moral blackmail that is unwilling, if not unwitting, to be found council homes.

> . . . there is now virtually no reasonably priced rented accommodation for a family with children to be got on the open market. Recently 45 young trainees, educated and articulate, spent a day searching for an unfurnished flat for a family with two children. Over 300 man-hours of systematic and intensive search failed to produce one flat. Three social workers working with large numbers of families in desperate housing need found four dwellings in the open market in three months. It is perhaps not surprising therefore that when a family loses its home (perhaps by illegal eviction) it fails to find another. [25]

No wonder such families eventually turn to emergency help. Temporary accommodation must remain the substitute for flexibility in the housing market until another substitute is found; and as the private rental market is further restricted, and as acute scarcity reduces what little flexibility and turnover remains, the problem of homelessness seems to be getting worse and worse. The councils, under this immense short-term pressure, are forced either to buy up the remaining private accommodation to house the homeless (making next year's homeless even less likely to find something) or to return to the private sector at a huge cost, by lodging them in bed-and-breakfast hotels! Until councils have begun to solve their long-term housing problem, they are powerless to solve the short-term one.

Housing and deprivation

Households, especially families, living in sub-standard housing are commonly referred to with the general label 'deprived', and indeed they are. But one final question is whether their deprivation consists mainly, or only, in their poor housing, or whether their poor housing is a consequence of deprivation in other fields, especially income and employment. The question turns out to be exceedingly difficult to answer from the statistics available. We can immediately agree that the better-off half of society in *housing* (owner-occupiers) is in general also the better-off half in *income*. But the term deprived is used to refer not to the lower half of society but to a much more isolated group. Are the worst-off for housing also the worst-off for income? Table 24 suggests that they are.

Table 24   Gross income of head of household by housing problems, 1973[26]

	Without sole use of a bath or shower (per cent)	*Without sole use of a W.C. inside the accommodation (per cent)*	*All households (per cent)*
Up to £10	28	32	16
£10-£20	28	26	19
£20-£30	23	22	21
£30-£50	18	18	31
Over £50	3	3	12

Most heads of household with an income below £20 are, however, old-age pensioners. As we have seen, these do live in poor housing, but for reasons connected with their generation rather than their age and retirement. Their low income is therefore coincidental with, rather than a cause of, poor housing. Eliminating old people from the analysis would much reduce the strength of the apparent relation; although there is a general tendency for lower incomes to mean poor housing, the proportion of the poor facilities experienced by better-off people is not negligible, and vice versa.

Clearly, facing an identical free-market situation, the better-off family will tend to secure better housing. But the immediate situation is probably far more important than income as a determinant of housing. An unskilled under-employed worker who has lived all his life in an area with plenty of houses will do far better than an affluent worker recently arrived in London. Moreover, council housing often neutralises the free-market forces altogether, by showing preference to the worst-off, at the expense of those more likely to fend for themselves. So a recent survey in Bethnal Green found no correlation at all between housing stress and low income, since the market was dominated by the council.[27]

This lack of correlation may well be a good deal less true for particular types of people, although it is not easy to find data to support the hypothesis. But it may be that certain minorities – coloured people, unmarried mothers, sick people, and so on – find it extra difficult both to obtain a good job and to find good housing. Again, it is not specifically low income that leads to poor housing, but since the same social abnormality causes both problems, we can conclude that the two are related.

There is not much comfort or hope for a family that has to endure both housing stress and low income; where the two are combined, there is a clear need for help. In general, though, it seems that the two are not so closely associated as the principles of free-market economics might lead one to expect – with the most important exception of the elderly. For poor families this is a relief; for better-off families that nevertheless suffer poor housing it must be a surprising frustration. It is some years now since people began to feel that income inequality, however desirable or inevitable it was in general, should not lead to housing inequality, at least within the rented sector. Partly, this means that there should be no bad housing; and partly that income should not be the determinant of who gets what housing. Already this latter aim is being achieved; as councils take over more of the rented sector, as more people have their rents paid by the social security, as rent and rate rebates become both more widespread and more generous, income is going to become less and less important in the allocation of housing in the rented sector. From the point of view of the poorest, whose allocation has previously been on the basis of ability to pay rent, this trend will undoubtedly be desirable: it has even been suggested that they should in future be allocated the very best accommodation as compensation for their other problems.

Nevertheless, it is possible to show that there are certain demographically definable groups in the population who have far more than their share of the nation's housing problems (Table 25). And these are the same groups as are known to have more than their share of all sorts of other problems.

Table 25 Housing problems of certain groups[28]

	Unskilled head of household	Semi-skilled head of household	Small elderly household	'Coloured' head of household	All house-holds
	(per cent)	(per cent)	(per cent)	(per cent)	(per cent)
Rent unfurnished	16	14	18	8	11
Rent furnished	3	3	1	18	3
Lack enough bedrooms	8	8	ϕ	25	6
Share or lack bath	21	18	17	29	12
Share or lack an inside W.C.			20	29	5

Thus, although low income itself does not seem to be the only or even the main determinant of bad housing, those groups in the population that are known to have low incomes are found to be most likely to have poor houses, presumably because for one reason or another they have been excluded from the opportunity of buying their houses, and perhaps even renting from the council. This conclusion is entirely in line with the suggestion in the Introduction to this report that deprivation may be considered as social accidents to which particular groups in the population are especially prone.

NOTES

1 Sources: (a) Dept. of the Environment, *National House Condition Survey 1971* (England & Wales); (b) 1971 Census, Housing Tables, part IV (England and Wales); (c) O.P.C.S., *General Household Survey 1971* (England and Wales); (d) 1971 Census, Housing Tables, Part II (England & Wales).

2 Sources: (a) Dept. of the Environment, *National House Condition Surveys 1967* and *1971*; (b-e) O.P.C.S., *General Household Survey 1971, op. cit.*

3 See e.g. B. Hedges, R. Berthoud, D. Bissonet and M. Wilson, *Housing in Westminster in 1972,* Westminster City Council/Social and Community Planning Research, 1974.

4 Dept. of the Environment, *Housing and Construction Statistics,* quarterly series.

5 *Ibid.*

6 Hedges *et al, op. cit.*

7 J. McCarthy, *Some Social Implications of Improvement Policy in London.* D.o.E. (1975).

8 D.o.E., *Housing and Construction Statistics, op. cit.*

9 Alvin L. Schorr, 'Housing Policy and Poverty', in P. Townsend (ed.), *The Concept of Poverty,* Heinemann Educational Books, 1970.

10 Central Statistical Office, *Social Trends, No. 4,* H.M.S.O., 1973.

11 *Ibid.*

12 *Ibid.*

13 O.P.C.S., *General Household Survey 1971, op. cit.*

14 J. Greve, *London's Homeless,* Bell, 1964.

15 Sources: *Social Trends, op. cit.,* and data supplied by G.L.C. The London figures include direct rehousing of homeless families, as well as admissions to temporary accommodation; an administrative change in that respect explains the outstanding leap between 1971 and 1972.

16 See J. Greve, D. Page and S. Greve, *Homelessness in London,* Scottish Academic Press, 1971. See also various reports and tracts issued by Shelter.

17 O.P.C.S., *General Household Survey, 1973,* H.M.S.O., 1976.

18 Sources: (a) *National House Condition Survey 1971, op. cit.*; (b-g) O.P.C.S., *General Household Survey 1973, op. cit.*

19 O.P.C.S., *General Household Survey 1973, op. cit.*

20 These figures are derived as follows:

    1 According to the census, there are 1,085,000 households with more than three persons in unfurnished privately rented accommodation (England & Wales).

    2 According to the *General Household Survey* (of 1971, the same date as the census), households containing three or more persons in unfurnished accommodation (Great Britain) divide

into small families, large families and large adult households in the proportions 46, 16 and 38 per cent respectively.

3 46 per cent of 1,085,000 is 499,000; and so on.

21 O.P.C.S., *General Household Survey 1971, op. cit.*

22 Hedges *et al., op. cit.*

23 B. Adams, *Some Social Problems of Housing,* Dept. of the Environment, unpublished, 1973.

24 O.P.C.S., *General Household Survey 1973, op. cit.*

25 B. Adams, *op. cit.*

26 O.P.C.S., *General Household Survey 1973, op. cit.*

27 L. Syson and M. Young, 'Poverty in Bethnal Green', in M. Young (ed.), *Poverty Report 1974,* Maurice Temple Smith, 1974.

28 O.P.C.S., *General Household Survey 1973, op. cit.*: the group identified in this table as small elderly households combines the G.H.S. 'Older small households' with 'Individuals aged 60 or over'.

4 Children

The aspect of deprivation that seems to cause most concern to society is its effects on children. As much as anything this may be because most, if unfortunately not all, of us feel an automatic love for children that is too often lacking for our fellow adults. Any book whose cover depicts children – the grubbier the better – attracts interest. The organisation currently leading the fight against all forms of poverty is called the *Child* Poverty Action Group, even though it does not confine its interest to children. There is, however, more to our concern over children than simply emotions or public relations.

Firstly, the existence of children in the family can often make the difference between hardship and poverty. There are many ways in which this works. The cost of feeding children may stretch low earnings too far; the need to care for them may prevent women from working to increase the household income or, in the case of unsupported mothers, they may prevent any earnings coming into the home at all; they can stand in the way of the search for adequate housing; or sometimes they may reduce the flexibility of their fathers in seeking work.

The second reason for special concern for children lies in their innocence. Whether low wages or skimpy social security benefits are intended as a punishment for idleness or as an unfortunately necessary incentive for productive work, they are directed against the parents; children play no part in the calculation, and it seems unfair that they should suffer because their fathers cannot obtain a better job.

Thirdly, because children cannot understand their situation, they may sometimes suffer more than their parents from any hardship they have in common. Conversely, the efforts of the parents to 'do right' by their children may lead them to forfeit many things, even food, which they otherwise might afford for themselves.

But the fourth reason is perhaps the most important. Both because the child is father to the man, and because childhood is an extremely vulnerable time of life, hardship in childhood may lead to a permanent injury to health, prosperity and happiness. Not only are today's deprived children most likely to be tomorrow's deprived adults, but, because they will also be tomorrow's deprived parents, many people consider the children as a key link in the continuing chain of deprivation.

The cycle of deprivation

This concern has been formulated theoretically as the 'cycle of deprivation'. The bare bones of the theory state simply that deprived people are descended from deprived parents, and in turn their descendants will be deprived. The fact of intergenerational continuity in the structure of society is scarcely a new phenomenon, nor a new observation. For centuries, even millenia, this would have been explained (if it was explained at all) either in terms of genetic inheritance (in pre-Darwinian terms, as 'blood') or in terms of divine ordination. Genetical theories are still put forward today, often by scientists with little understanding of social mechanisms, and rejected out of hand by social commentators who may never have heard of Mendel. Even the doctrine of grace may still be recognised today in the attitudes of many towards the continuing structure of inequality. While it is almost certain that biological inheritance plays some part in social behaviour, we are a long way from knowing with any certainty how great that part is. It is abundantly clear that there is a great range in individuals' intrinsic abilities, and that part at least of that variation can be explained in terms of the parents' abilities. It may also be that most of those who rise to the very top of the social tree have exceptional abilities, while most of those who fall to the very bottom lack such talents. But it is by no means certain that the pattern of status really matches the pattern of ability. To take an example from a field where genetic influences are well known, it is certain that Mozart had a great talent, but not certain that other little boys might not have been just as brilliant if there had been a piano in their home. Social and structural influences must be as important, therefore, as genetical ones; moreover, society can hope to change the social factors, while it can have no influence on the genetic unless we resort to controlled breeding. The only practical purpose of measures of the genetic influence on deprivation would seem to be, therefore, in justifying the *status quo* rather than in seeking to change it.

Among social factors three types are currently the subject of discussion. Perhaps the oldest in history, but with only a recent theoretical expression, is that poor people are fitted for poverty by their early experience of it, so that either through knowing their place, or through an induced sense of hopelessness, they lack the *motivation* to push their way up the social ladder.

The second theory is that whoever the person, and whatever his abilities or determination, society imposes external structural barriers that prevent people brought up in one class from progressing to a higher class. Historically such barriers have clearly been of key importance, and many of the social reforms in post-industrial society, especially the provision of universal educational opportunity, have been attempts to dismantle them.

For a long time it was thought that a universal education system would provide a simple key to all social doors. It may yet provide a key, but we have discovered that it will not be a simple one; for since education has been provided for all children, it has been found that it has not had the expected effect of reducing the educational gap between children from different strata in society. So a third theory has been developed, which is of most direct relevance to our present discussion of children. This theory, closely associated with the label 'cycle of deprivation', suggests that being brought up in a deprived home prevents the full development of a child's potential abilities, so that he is not in a position to take advantage of schooling. The problem is, in the current jargon, inadequate socialisation.

The basic outline of the theory of the deprivation cycle is shown in Fig. 3.[1] It is cyclical in that the characteristic of the parent in the top left-hand corner is linked to the same characteristic in the next generation of parents in the bottom right-hand corner. The simple part of the cycle is seen in the series of links a, b, c and d. Without defining exactly what 'social characteristics' mean, let us assume them to include a low level of job skill.

(a) A low level of job skills limits the choice of employment to unskilled jobs, or even causes unemployment.

(b) A poor job or unemployment produces a low income.

(c) Low income limits housing choice, and often leads to poor

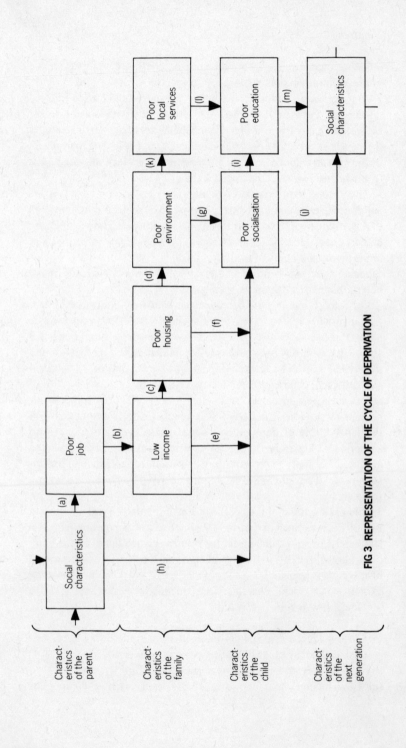

FIG 3   REPRESENTATION OF THE CYCLE OF DEPRIVATION

housing, although, as we have seen (p.101), the link between low income and poor housing is by no means a simple one.

(d) Poor housing is often to be found clustered together in unsatisfactory areas.

Each of these intermediate effects is thought to have an effect on the development (or socialisation) of the child.

(e) Low income means that the parents have to spend long hours either at their job or on the housework (washing clothes by hand, perhaps), so that they have little time or temper to devote to the children. Secondly, there is no money to spare on toys, crayons, books, outings etc., which are essential to the child's development.

(f) Poor housing often means crowded housing, where the children lack privacy and play space, and where heavy discipline may be necessary to prevent pandemonium.

(g) A poor environment may mean nowhere to play, or playing beyond the control of parents.

All these things, singly and collectively, may well severely inhibit a child's emotional and mental development. On the other hand, these links in the chain *could* all be broken by the beneficent interference of government, through income support, housing policy, or town planning. It is not so easy, however, to see how government can interfere with the apparent direct link between the social characteristics of the parent and the socialisation of the child, which is often held to be the most important single factor.

(h) The theory is that the life style of working-class parents (in turn derived from their own parents) is, by comparison with middle-class parents, not suited to the child's development. Working-class parents are different in their approach to their children. They are held to be less child-centred; they spend less time on the children; and they exert discipline for their own sake (keeping the child quiet), not for the child's long-term sake (forming his character).[2] Secondly, either because they do not spend time talking to the child, or because, when they do, they use a particular speech pattern, the children's own linguistic ability is slow to develop. The restricted language of the child in turn hinders the development of his thought processes, so that by the time he reaches school he is already at a serious disadvantage.[3]

It is important to note that, in this summary of the theory, the terms 'working class' and 'middle class' have been used without definition. It is very often not clear from the literature whether the distinction depends on the father's occupation or on the parents' cultural behaviour. It sometimes seems that conclusions based on one definition are used to derive inferences based on another. Nor is it clear how sharp the division between middle and working class is – whether all members of each class exhibit a particular set of characteristics, or whether there is a degree of overlap – nor yet whether the distinction is simply between one and the other, or whether there is a continuum between *very* middle class at one end and *very* working class at the other, with an indeterminate group in the middle. Nor is it clear why a characteristic held to be 'working class' – i.e. applying to two-thirds of the population – should explain the circumstances of the deprived, who constitute a small minority. All these points will be discussed in the concluding chapter: for the purposes of the remainder of this discussion of socialisation, a simple distinction will be assumed between the characteristics of the top end of the middle class, and those of the bottom end of the working class.

The theory of socialisation and the effects of parental behaviour (or rather, the set of theories) is, of course, far more complicated than the brief explanation above can indicate – the explanation scarcely does it justice. To the layman it may sometimes seem that the evidence of general tendencies may not justify the heavy inevitability implied in the conclusions. For instance, as every middle-class parent knows, keeping children quiet by threats or bribery is not an exclusively working-class practice. Again it is not obvious why the observed difference between the linguistic styles of middle-class and working-class children should have such enormous consequences. Typically, working-class children telling a story based on a set of pictures will assume that the listener is also looking at the pictures; they use pronouns instead of nouns, saying, for instance, *'They're playing football and he kicks it'*. Middle-class children, however, tell the story with enough nouns for the non-observer to understand: *'Three boys are playing football and one boy kicks the ball'*.[4]

Again, it is not always clear just how typical of each class are the characteristics assigned to it. For instance, it has been found, on the one hand, that most, but not all, upper middle-class parents show a 'liberal' response to sexual curiosity, while most, but not all, lower working-class parents show a 'puritan' response.[5] On the other hand, much has been made of the finding that middle-class parents are relatively likely to accept the excuse that the child is 'busy' when he or she is asked to perform some chore. But the fact remains that while more than three-quarters of the middle-class parents exhibited this characteristic; so too did around two-thirds of the working-class parents.[6] The tendency is scarcely sufficient to justify inferences based on 'typical' behaviour.

To some observers both these examples may suggest that perhaps socialisation theory depends in part on researchers observing characteristics in middle-class parental behaviour of which they – the middle-class researchers – approve, and that the inferred consequences are little more than a justification for currently fashionable modes of upbringing. After all, it could be argued, the 'puritan' response to sexual curiosity did not do much harm to the children of the original 'Puritans' – so far as we know, it did not undermine faith in the honesty and authority of adults, nor did it lead to cultural or material deprivation in the next generation. On the other hand, questioning the inferential validity of the theory in this way does not serve to contradict the essential facts on which it is based. The facts are that there is an observed correlation between (a) the material circumstances of parents, (b) the socio-cultural characteristics of the parents, (c) the preliminary development of the child, (d) the performance of the child at school and (e) the social status of the child when he reaches adulthood. Of course, none of these correlations is anywhere near perfect; the exception may be so frequent as to deny the existence of a 'rule'. Nevertheless, from these correlations hypotheses about causal relations need to be formulated, while it is admitted that there is bound to be a good deal of the chicken and egg problem to be coped with.

There seem to be two basic hypotheses implicit in the discussion of these relations (Fig. 4). One hypothesis starts with the socio-cultural characteristics of the parent, and suggests that these cause two consequences independently: firstly, the material circumstances of the home, and, secondly, the parental behaviour which leads to poor socialisation. On this basis any direct effect of reduced material circumstances of the child is relegated to a secondary role. According to the alternative hypothesis, it is the material situation that is of first consequence to the parental behaviour and the child's development, while the original socio-cultural characteristics of the parent are reduced to, at most, a catalytic function.

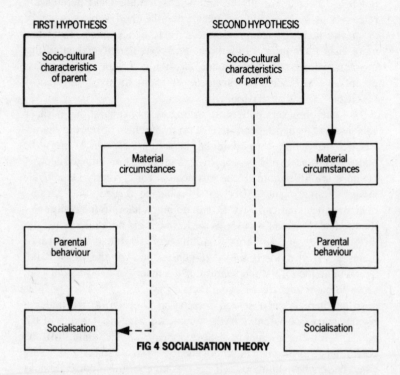

FIG 4 SOCIALISATION THEORY

There is no proof for either of these hypotheses, either way. The author believes that the second sounds more credible than the first. Unfortunately, the first hypothesis sometimes seems to be used to imply that deprivation is caused by the personal problems of those who get into it; while the second is used to imply that the personal problems are a consequence of a society that imposes deprivation on some of its members. The question of where the 'blame' lies should be irrelevant to any decision on *whether* the deprived deserve help; it is relevant, if at all, only to a decision on *how* they can be helped. And since there is an observed relation between deprivation and education, which is a public responsibility, it is worth seeing if education can play any role in getting rid of the problem.

Large families

Before we go on to consider the role of the school in the process, we should go back over the ground already covered, to consider the position not just of the typical child but of the child in an exceptionally large family. There are only about 215,000 families in Great Britain with five or more dependent children, just over 1 per cent of all households, or 3 per cent of all families with dependent children.[7] The number would be greater if we added in those that will be large when more children are born, or used to be large before elder children became independent. But there are signs that large families are on the decrease. The proportion of Family Allowance families with five or more children fell from 6.0 per cent to 3.9 per cent between 1966 and 1974;[8] perhaps a more sensitive indicator is the number of babies born to mothers of four previous children, which fell steadily from 55,700 in 1966 to 16,500 in 1974,[9] and is still falling.

Before showing how large families tend to be deprived, it is useful to see whether deprived families tend to be large. It is possible to say that the families of manual workers are at least twice as likely to be large as the families of non-manual workers – and the lower the skill level, the greater the likelihood. Nevertheless, large families are a tiny minority even for unskilled workers. Table 26 refers to families with five or more dependent children.

Table 26 Incidence of large families, by social class[10]

Managerial/ Professional	Other non- manual	Skilled manual	Semi- skilled	Unskilled
1½%	1½%	3%	4%	7%

It is not, therefore, possible to say that 'the working classes' are 'feckless breeders'. If we were particularly anxious about inability to limit family size, we could say that it was *on the whole* a lower working-class phenomenon, and we could draw two conclusions: that lower working-class access to family planning services should be improved (cultural access, as much as physical access); and that if fecklessness is the cause of large families, there is no reason to believe that a large increase in Family Allowances would encourage overpopulation.

Nevertheless, the social consequences of having a large family are much clearer than the social causes; for the existence of too many brothers and sisters seems to have an amplifying effect on a number of the factors in the cycle of deprivation already discussed. The letters heading the paragraphs below refer again to the links in the cycle in Fig. 3, p. 108.

(b) *Low income.* Obviously, the more children in the family, the more stretched the family budget; social security has only a marginal alleviating effect, except for those families that are already very poor. Secondly, a long period of child-bearing means a long period when the mother's earning opportunities are severely limited. Low income becomes more serious as time goes on.

(c) *Housing.* It seems a truism that large families will live in crowded conditions. Thus, even when 'large' is defined as three or more children, 20 per cent of large families have one bedroom fewer than they 'need', and 3 per cent fall short of their needs by two or more; while over half of all other households have at least one bedroom to spare.[11] But, of course, this need not be so. The problem is at least as much one of the size of the house as of the size of the family. Only 3 per cent of council homes have more than three bedrooms[12] (compared with 8 per cent private rental and $13\frac{1}{2}$ per cent owner-occupied), so that large families simply cannot be catered for.

But the key factor again seems to be the micro-society within the home.

(h) *Socialisation.* The greater the number of children, the more time the mother must spend on housework, and the remaining time must be divided between more children; communication is restricted to essentials, discipline becomes more strictly necessary, intersibling rivalry (children quarrelling) more intense. Even totally new problems arise: some children from large families may arrive at school with no experience of sitting down to table for a proper meal, because there was no table big enough at home.[13]

Thus, whatever the social class, children from large families have been shown to be less adapted for school than those from small ones; and the effect on the early years is demonstrated by the greater handicap applying to the younger children.

Education

If we return to the chart of the cycle of deprivation (Fig. 3), we can look at the role schooling is often thought to play in all this.

(k) Deprived families living in deprived areas are held to suffer from poor provision of local services, especially, in this instance, poor schools. The inadequacy of the schools may rest in their physical structure (old, crowded etc.) or in their teaching (underqualified staff, high turnover, low teacher-pupil ratio etc.).
(l) The poor quality of the school is held in turn to hinder the child's school progress.

Both these hypotheses seem eminently plausible. The first is constantly being asserted by those concerned with education in deprived areas. The second surely *must* be true; if bad schools or bad teachers do not provide bad education, what is the point of wasting money on good schools and good teachers?

The Plowden Council on primary schools,[14] whose own research provided further evidence of the link between social and educational disadvantage, based its principal recommendations on precisely this pair of hypotheses – that the socially disadvantaged children suffered from poor schooling, and that better schooling would enable them to get a better education. They therefore recommended that socially disadvantaged areas should be sought out, and the schools in those areas should be offered preferential treatment in salary increases, building grants and so on, in order to bring them well up to the standard of schools elsewhere. This Educational Priority Area policy has been adopted, though perhaps not with the financial muscle appropriate to so large a problem. (When one thinks about it, the process of locating schools for special help by finding *areas* of multiple deprivation, on the basis that deprived children are likely to do badly at school, is rather a roundabout method. It necessitates attempting to combine the data on various socio-economic variables into a single indicator. Why not a more direct approach – give special help to those schools whose children are of lowest measured achievement?)

This 'try harder' policy is certainly necessary, in the absence of any other workable solution to the poor educational achievement of deprived children. It is curious, however, that it is based on two hypotheses which, though obviously reasonable, resolutely refuse to be proved by any statistical analysis. The Plowden Council itself, for instance, did not establish any link between social characteristics and school characteristics (link h in Fig. 3): judging from the published research report, they do not seem to have attempted it statistically, although the right sorts of data were available, and the main Council report asserted that the link existed. In fact, whatever the quality of the schools in the areas, it has since been found that the concentration of 'deprived' children in 'deprived' areas is not sufficient to justify an area-based approach – most deprived children live outside such areas, and most children in such areas are not deprived.[15] Secondly, the Council's research indicated that variations in school characteristics had very little effect on the achievement of the pupils (link l) – between nil and 11 per cent of the variation in performance, compared with between 19 per cent and 35 per cent attributable to attitudes of the parents.[16]

More recent data continue perversely to refute the obvious. Highly deprived 11-year-olds attend schools with average-aged buildings, average teacher-turnover, and below-average size of class. But in spite of being at least average in their schooling, they continue to be below average in their attainment.[17] Innumerable attempts to establish a relation between class size and attainment have succeeded, only to find that larger classes appear to have *better* than average results. Indeed, the principal conclusion of an exhaustive, if controversial, review of the (American) evidence suggests that different schools make little, if any, difference to the educational success of their pupils: the observed differences in performance are almost entirely explained in terms of differences in the quality of the intake.[18]

The fact that we cannot prove in advance that the E.P.A. policy ought to work does not, of course, mean that it will not work, or that direct evaluation of the policy's effects will not show that it has worked. The direct research on the policy is not clear in its conclusions: one report shows that the educational innovations did not achieve what their instigators felt they had achieved:[19] another report suggests that the E.P.A. programme would have useful long-term effects if combined with a wider-ranging active social policy.[20] We ought, therefore, to seek other strings to our bow. Most importantly, the comparative failure of deprived children, whatever the school, suggests that the main problem is at home – as socialisation theory also suggests. In fact, the second main string to the

Plowden Council's bow was based on their finding (quoted above) that the single general factor most closely related to children's performance was parental attitudes (aspiration for child, literacy of home and parental interest in school work and progress).

This policy was concerned with forging closer links between the home and the school. For, in spite of the new relaxed atmosphere within primary school classrooms,* a formal relation continues between home and school. There are still two quite independent environments with which the child has to cope, perhaps exemplified by the acute embarrassment many children feel when they meet their teacher while out with their mother. And the separation of these environments may constitute more of a problem for the low-status than the high-status child. A new co-operation between mother and teacher must be found, but it will not be easy. Setting more times for parents to come to talk to their children's teachers will be a step in the right direction, but it is scarcely a solution to the problem. It is difficult for parents who remember the formality of the relationship with their own teachers, who did badly at school themselves or who know little of modern educational practice, to develop an easy relation with the teacher. Nor is it easy for the teacher who has to cope every year with perhaps forty new parents, who may be sensitive to implied criticism, who may not have experienced hardship herself or who (knowing something of socialisation theory) may see herself as trying to educate the child in spite of his parental handicap! Of course, however good the relation, there are some aspects of home life – the literacy of the parents, for instance – which are not immediately affected by it. Nevertheless, a recognition by both sides that education is a joint effort would surely help.

But the most critical period of a child's life occurs in the five years before he starts attending school. Is there any way in which society can assist in the socialisation process during that period, without interfering with family freedom? Adequate material circumstances are certainly one goal to aim at. Secondly, after thirty years of lamentable lack of effort, there are strong signs that government is

---

* This relaxation is not yet complete. For instance, teacher may be, for many children, their only daily contact addressed solely by surname. Nor, for that matter, has it been proved that the more relaxed atmosphere is conducive to educational progress for the deprived. Recent research indicates that formal teaching is better for all except low ability boys, but unfortunately there is no analysis of those with deprived home backgrounds who were considered to be so important by the Plowden Council.[21]

about to provide nursery schooling for the children of all parents who want it. Those active in nursery schooling have always felt that it has helped, but it is by no means certain that any advantage is prolonged beyond about the first year of primary schooling. Nor is it obvious why universal nursery schooling should narrow the class gap any more effectively than did universal primary or secondary schooling in the past. Moreover, if it is voluntary, will it help those children who need it most – those whose parents take little interest in their education? In short, there is no obvious easy way to ensure that deprived infants are able to obtain the fullest benefit from primary school.

Of course, the conclusion that deprived children are not suited for school is only one implication to be drawn from the evident dissonance between school and home. We could argue that the dissonance arises from the attempt to apply middle-class schooling, with middle-class aspirations, to working-class children: that it is not the socialisation process that requires modification, but the school that needs to be brought into line with working-class culture.

This problem is easily raised, and it has found practical expression in the recent development of 'free schools'. But it is not easy to discuss in terms of its policy implications. In the first place, if socialisation theory is correct in characterising working-class culture as lacking a developed time-continuum – as a reluctance to postpone present pleasure for future gratification – then working-class culture is completely at odds with the whole concept of education, based as it is on a child's work for the adult's success. Secondly, if teaching is by its nature a middle-class occupation, teachers will be middle-class, and will purvey a middle-class culture. Perhaps that second point is simply a restatement of the first.

In spite of these theoretical objections we can ask what sort of change in school culture might tend to lessen the apparent gap between it and working-class culture. In primary schools perhaps that sort of change has already taken place, or is still in progress, in the more relaxed atmosphere, the greater emphasis on general develop-ment, and the reduced emphasis on syllabus, achievement and competitive success. And the recent freedom from anxiety about 'getting pupils through' the 11-plus may well bring about further improvement along these lines.

In secondary schools, however, it is another story, whatever changes may have taken place in teaching methods; for the secondary school's most important practical role continues to be to sort adolescents into hierarchical grades, so that each shall know what rung in society's ladder he is destined for. The entire secondary school process, from the working-class child's point of view, is to identify those who cannot pass any exams, those who can get one or two CSEs or O-levels, those who can obtain several O-levels, those who can get A-levels, and those who can go to university. Schools have been described as 'certification agencies'.[22] Whatever the relevance of the subjects studied to 'life' or to work, it is these qualifications that will mainly determine the rank in society to which he will belong. At least, so he is told at school. And it is on that basis that we continue to measure the success or failure of education in modifying the life chances of the working class. Looked at in this way, we can see secondary education as perhaps more of a barrier to social mobility than a gateway through the barrier; for, just as socialisation theory predicts, the class gap already existing in primary schools suddenly and finally widens at secondary school, with its greater emphasis on syllabus, learning and achievement. Not only do deprived children tend not to do so well, but even the comparatively successful ones may lose interest, fail to attend regularly, and leave without the qualifications they might have obtained.

Part of this difference between primary and secondary schooling can be seen in terms of the adult chauvinism that continues to affect teenagers, from which younger children have been partly emancipated. At the beginning of this chapter it was suggested that we feel an automatic love for a small child, however grubby. Do we feel the same way about that child's elder brother, as he loses his innocence?

This worry about the suitability of secondary education for both middle- and working-class children is not new. Thirty years ago it led to a splitting of secondary education into academic and practical schools (grammar and secondary modern), with its polite assumption that those without academic ability would have a practical ability that should be developed. There was also a polite assertion that there would be no distinction between working-class and middle-class children except on innate ability. We now know, of course, that there *was* a distinction, not necessarily a conscious one but, if socialisation theory is correct, an inevitable one. The quandary is this: if working-class children are to be offered an education peculiarly fitted to working-class culture, we automatically deprive them of the qualifications that would allow them to reach greater prosperity or more interesting work – that is, so long as those qualifications are necessary to prosperity.

Of course, for the great majority of non-professional jobs, the particular educational qualifications required are not peculiarly appropriate. They are used, in the absence of peculiar qualifications, as a proxy for general ability. Some other proxy might do equally well, perhaps some form of qualification for which deprived children are not at such a disadvantage. The main system of qualifications we use today is peculiarly suited to measure potential ability at university–it is even administered by the universities. University is the highest summit of educational aspiration. So long as universities continue to recruit direct from school on the basis of school results (which some people think is a bad idea anyway), secondary schools, and employers, and the whole social structure, are bound to rely on qualifications geared solely towards measuring academic ability.

Multiply-deprived children

So far this chapter has contained more chat than fact. The facts illustrating the problem of the deprived child have been saved to the end, because they have been dramatically presented from a single source, the *National Child Development Study,* [23] in which 10,500 children born in one week in 1958 have been the subject of repeated study–most recently at the age of 11. From the sample three basic dimensions of disadvantage were isolated:

1 *Family structure:* children with four or more brothers and sisters *or* with only one parent.
2 *Low income:* children receiving free school meals *or* Supplementary Benefit.
3 *Housing:* overcrowded (over one and a half persons per room) *or* lacking hot water.

On these criteria 23 per cent of 11-year-olds had an imbalanced family structure, 14 per cent had families with low income (a likely underestimate, because of non-take-up of free school meals), and 23 per cent lived in poor housing.

Of all the 11-year-olds, 36 per cent had at least one of these problems. *Six per cent had all three problems combined.* But it was in the long catalogue of special problems that these hard-core

disadvantaged children faced that the concept of Multiple Deprivation was first given real meaning.

The study compared children with *all* these disadvantages with
those who had *none* of them (referred to as ordinary – 64 per cent of
all the children). In the following paragraphs, the figures in brackets
give first the proportion of 'disadvantaged' children with a given
characteristic, and second the proportion of 'ordinary' children with
that characteristic.

They were more likely to have been born to teenaged mothers (7 per
   cent: 4 per cent).
They were more likely to have mothers who were less than 5 feet tall
   (5 per cent: 2 per cent) or who smoked heavily during pregnancy
   (19 per cent: 10 per cent).
Their mothers tended not to make an antenatal visit during the first 15
   weeks of pregnancy (70 per cent: 42 per cent), nor to make more
   than four antenatal visits altogether (10 per cent: 3 per cent), nor to
   make a booking for their confinement (2.5 per cent: 0.4 per cent).
Partly as a result, they were more likely to be born prematurely (25
   per cent: 17 per cent), and to weigh $5\frac{1}{2}$ lb or less at birth (8 per cent:
   5 per cent).

As well as the housing problems already contained within the
definition of deprivation (crowding and/or lacking hot water), there
were other problems at home:

They tended to have no bathroom (17 per cent: 2 per cent) or indoor
   lavatory (25 per cent: 6 per cent).
They were remarkably likely to share a bed (not just a bedroom) with
   other children (53 per cent: 9 per cent). Some of them both shared a
   bed *and wet it,* at the age of 11 (4.5 per cent: 0.4 per cent).

Not surprisingly, the children's parents were most unlikely to have
middle-class (non-manual) occupations; and, as the socialisation
theory would lead us to expect, their parents were comparatively
unlikely to have had more than the minimum of education. Their
reading habits were also comparatively slight. But the children could
point to more specific disadvantages among their parents:

Both their mother (11 per cent: 5 per cent) and their father (17 per cent: 4.5 per cent) were more likely to have chronic or serious ill-health than 'ordinary' children's.

Their fathers were likely to have been off work sick in the previous year (50 per cent: 28 per cent), many of them for more than 20 weeks (18 per cent: 1.5 per cent) or even for the whole year (9.5 per cent: 0.2 per cent).

Similarly, their fathers tended to have been unemployed during the previous year (34 per cent: 3 per cent), often for more than 20 weeks (19 per cent: 0.4 per cent) or for the whole year (8.5 per cent: 0.03 per cent).

The children themselves had far more than their fair share of specific health or development problems:

They were likely to be short (under 4 feet 7 inches at age 11: 42 per cent: 18 per cent).

They were more accident-prone, both to burns and scalds (14 per cent: 9 per cent) and to serious flesh wounds (4 per cent: 1 per cent).

They were more prone to serious illnesses such as rheumatic fever, infectious hepatitis, meningitis or tuberculosis (6 per cent: 3 per cent).

Many of them had missed between 1 and 3 months of school in the previous year (9 per cent: 4 per cent) or even more than 3 months (2 per cent: 0.4 per cent).

They had difficulties in hearing (2.9 per cent: 0.7 per cent) or in speaking (4.6 per cent: 1.5 per cent).

Many of them were said to be educationally sub-normal (5 per cent: 0.7 per cent).

Again, as socialisation theory would lead us to expect, the disadvantaged children's parents seemed to take comparatively little interest in their schooling:

They tended not to have visited the school to talk to their child's teacher (61 per cent: 35 per cent).

They were comparatively likely to want their child to leave school as soon as possible (17 per cent: 3 per cent), though two-thirds hoped for further education for their child.

When it came to assessing the children's performance at school, the pattern remained unchanged:

Their teachers might assess their behaviour as 'disturbed' (29 per cent: 18 per cent) or even 'maladjusted' (26 per cent: 9 per cent), although, of course, this may reflect the teacher's attitude as much as the child's behaviour.
They were likely to be receiving 'special help' in the normal school (17 per cent: 6 per cent).
They scored poorly on a reading test (58 per cent: 21 per cent) and on a maths test (56 per cent: 22 per cent).

Finally, it is clear that, whereas these families make above average demands on various social services explicitly intended to help those with special problems, they made comparatively little use of services intended to help everybody. Thus, on the one hand:

The children tended to have been 'in care' at some time in their lives (11 per cent: 1 per cent).
The families tended to have been helped by children's departments (10 per cent: 0.3 per cent); mental health departments (4.5 per cent: 1.5 per cent); education departments (17 per cent: 1 per cent); or the probation service (9 per cent: 0.3 per cent).
The families tended to have been supported by sickness benefit (33 per cent: 17 per cent), unemployment benefit (25 per cent: 2 per cent) or a disability pension (4 per cent: 2 per cent), as well as by supplementary benefit and/or free school meals.
The children were receiving (or waiting to receive) special education (7 per cent: 1.3 per cent).

On the other hand:

As we have seen, antenatal services were less used by the mothers of deprived children.
So also, with infant welfare clinics: deprived children were taken irregularly (67 per cent: 33 per cent) or not at all (33 per cent: 20 per cent).
Finally, these children were likely not to have been immunised against polio (12.5 per cent: 2.5 per cent), diphtheria (14 per cent: 3 per cent) or smallpox (40 per cent: 20 per cent).

This appalling series of figures illustrates the central theme of this report – that the group of people who are afflicted with one set of problems are highly likely to suffer many others. But the association is never so close as to be ascribed to a direct cause and effect relation. Some, perhaps many, 'ordinary' children suffer each of these problems; many, perhaps most, 'deprived' children do not. If we cannot explain why Mary is short but Jane is not, then Mary's shortness will have to be seen as an 'accident' in much the same way as Jane's burns or scalds. The problem is that Mary and Jane seem to be more prone to all such accidents than Amanda and Joanna; and this problem, for all its social origins, seems to apply at least as much to physical health as to more clearly social factors.

Finally, we should beware of the temptation to interpret the fact that a particular cultural or behavioural phenomenon is more common in one section of society than another as meaning that it is a characteristic of that group, which in turn explains other apparent characteristics. For example, it is by now well known that the average reading ability of children from working-class homes is lower than that of children from middle-class homes (Table 27).

Table 27 Reading scores of 11-year-old children in Inner London by occupation of father, 1971 [24]

	Professional/ Managerial (per cent)	Other Non-manual (per cent)	Skilled Manual (per cent)	Semi- skilled (per cent)	Un- skilled (per cent)
Up to 83 points*	7	15	22	31	38
84 to 93 points*	13	21	25	26	27
94 to 104 points*	21	28	27	25	21
105 points or more*	58	36	25	18	14
Mean	107 pts	99 pts	95 pts	91 pts	88 pts

*83, 93 and 104 points are the quartiles of the distribution. If there were no class bias, there would be about 25 per cent in each cell of the table.

These figures, indicating that the average child of an unskilled father is about a year-and-a-half behind the average child of a professional or managerial father (one point is roughly equivalent to one month), provide a vivid illustration of the class gap in society, and demonstrate the need for a new educational solution. On the other hand, they do not at all show that working-class children are universally poor readers. Variations between individual children are so great that only 11 per cent of the variation can be attributed to social class differences; the remaining 89 per cent is attributable to differences between children within each group. As a result, there is only a little truth in the suggestion that middle-class children's life chances are better because they are able to do better at school.

NOTES

1 The literature contributing to theories of socialisation and of cycles of deprivation is vast. A good summary, with references, is Harriett Wilson, 'The Socialisation of Children', in R. Holman (ed.), *Socially Deprived Families in Britain*, Bedford Square Press, 1970. A comprehensive review is in M. Rutter and N. Madge, *Cycles of Deprivation, a review of research,* Heinemann, forthcoming.
2 See especially J. and E. Newson, *Infant Care in an Urban Community,* Allen & Unwin, 1963, and *Four Years Old in an Urban Community,* Allen & Unwin, 1968.
3 See especially the work of B. Bernstein, e.g. 'A Socio-linguistic Approach to Social Learning', in J. Gould (ed.), *Penguin Survey of the Social Sciences,* Penguin, 1965.
4 Quoted by B. Bernstein, in 'A Critique of the Concept of Compensatory Education', in D. Wedderburn (ed.), *Poverty, Inequality and Class Structure,* Cambridge U.P., 1974.
5 J. and E. Newson, *op. cit.* (1968).
6 *Ibid.*
7 1971 Census, Summary Tables (1 per cent sample).
8 Department of Health and Social Security, *Social Security Statistics 1974,* H.M.S.O.
9 Registrar General's *Quarterly Returns.*
10 1971 Census, *loc. cit.*
11 O.P.C.S., *General Household Survey 1973,* H.M.S.O.
12 *Ibid.*
13 H. Land, *Large Families in London,* Bell, 1969.
14 Central Advisory Council for Education (England), *Children and Their Primary Schools* (the Plowden Report), H.M.S.O., 1967.
15 J. H. Barnes and H. Lucas, 'Positive Discrimination in Education: Individuals, Groups and Institutions', in J. H. Barnes (ed.), *Educational Priority,* Vol 3, H.M.S.O., 1975.

16 Central Advisory Council for Education, *op. cit.*
17 P. Wedge and H. Prosser, *Born to Fail?,* Arrow Books, 1973.
18 C. Jencks *et al, Inequality,* Basic Books (U.S.), 1972; Allen Lane (G.B.), 1973.
19 J. H. Barnes, (ed.), *op. cit.*
20 G. Smith (ed.), *Educational Priority,* Vol 4, H.M.S.O., 1975.
21 N. Bennett, *Teaching Styles and Pupil Progress,* Open Books, 1976.
22 C. Jencks *et al, op. cit.*
23 P. Wedge and H. Prosser, *op. cit.* In the original text many of the proportions were expressed as fractions (e.g. 1 in 7). For the sake of uniformity in this précis they have been converted to percentages (e.g. 1 in 7=14 per cent), and the figures may not be precisely accurate (e.g. Wedge and Prosser could also have expressed 15 per cent as 1 in 7).
24 Data provided by I.L.E.A.'s research department, based on their own survey.

5 Employment

Considering the central importance of employment in determining both income and the status of a man and his family in society, there is a surprising lack of discussion of the subject in the literature on *personal* deprivation and poverty, although employment is at the centre of the discussion of deprived *areas*. Some reviews of the problems of deprivation do not consider the role of employment at all, taking low wages or the dole as an accepted cause of low income, and discussing only the problems of poverty arising in consequence. The feeling that low-status employment is a cause of deprivation, rather than an aspect of it about which action should be taken, is perhaps reinforced by the fact that socio-economic 'classes' in society are usually defined by job characteristics; any attempt to analyse the sorts of jobs held by people of different classes is therefore impossibly circular.

In this chapter specific deprivations in employment are considered in a roughly logical order: difficulties in getting jobs; problems experienced during employment; and problems arising as a consequence of employment. Not surprisingly, all the problems will be found to affect mainly, or even exclusively, the manual worker; at the end of the chapter, therefore, there will be a brief discussion of why this situation arises.

Unemployment[1]

The proportion of potential workers who are unemployed at any one time fluctuates between 2 per cent and 6 per cent of the workforce – an apparently small number in comparison with some of our other social problems, such as those affecting the elderly, but nevertheless representing very serious problems for perhaps 1,000,000 families. The long-term trend appears to be towards more and more unemployment. As we might expect from our knowledge of all the other problems which affect those of low social status, the risk of unemployment is least for managerial and professional workers, and greatest for the unskilled (Table 28).

Table 28   **Percentage male unemployment rates, by social class**[2]

Professionals, managers etc.	2.0
Other non-manual	3.0
Skilled manual	4.2
Semi-skilled manual	5.2
Unskilled manual	11.8

One of the few arguments offered positively in favour of unemployment is that it holds down inflation by weakening the bargaining position of those in work. It is by no means certain that it can have such an effect in the short term, but if it does, it can clearly be seen whose wages are most likely to be held down as a result.

It may be tempting to interpret the comparatively high incidence of unemployment.among the unskilled as indicating that the unemployed represent the least employable stratum of society; that when there are 1,000,000 unemployed, they are the 1,000,000 least 'valuable' out of work, to be re-employed when the total drops again. Up to a point, this interpretation has some value. Those without a formal skill, or with limited skills, are perhaps twice as common among the unemployed as among those in work. Similarly, those with long-standing health disadvantages are heavily over-represented among the unemployed. So, many of the least employable people are to be found among the unemployed. On the other hand, a great number of unemployed people are highly employable, in that they have demonstrated their ability to acquire and apply a skill or have held down a semi-skilled or unskilled job in the recent past, and are in satisfactory health. Moreover, unskilled and/or ill people are more common (in absolute numbers) in the workforce than out of it.

The explanation seems to be that there are many people in work who are quite capable of holding down a job as long as that job exists, but who for one reason or another are first on the list for the sack when employers find themselves overstaffed, and who, for those same reasons, experience difficulty in finding or adjusting to a new job once they have lost the old. They are not unemployable – had they not worked for an overstaffed employer, they could have carried on, and some of them do find a new job in the end – but once unemployed, they are in a weak position, which leaves them on the dole for a long time. The approach to a solution makes economic as well as social sense: as workers grow older and lose their health, they should be found jobs within the firm for which their health is not a disadvantage; when redundancies are inevitable, those (especially the young) who will experience least difficulty in re-employment should be released first; and finally, those whose age and health really does make them unemployable should be offered more humane, dignified and generous arrangements for 'retirement' instead of the poverty and stigma of the dole.

All this will be a good deal easier to propose than achieve. The economic position of the employer must be considered, for he has a loyalty to the whole workforce as well as to those of declining productivity. It is not suggested that employers need follow the example of aristocratic families who used to retain their nanny as a pensioner long after the children grew up. Nevertheless, some action along these lines is desirable; the Germans seem to be rather better in this respect than we are without any economic disaster ensuing.[3]

The lead has been given by the arrangements for non-manual and senior staff. Unemployment among the upper occupational groups is less common not only because they are on a good employment wicket, not only because managers find it difficult to sack their personal acquaintances, and not only because qualified personnel are difficult to reacquire after a period of recession. Part of their good fortune lies in their conditions of service. Ill-health is much less of a disadvantage for non-manual workers, and the more senior positions held by older men are often least active of all. When sackings are made, staff are usually given at least a month's notice in which to seek another job, and often a fairly generous payment to tide them over any period out of work. Finally, when staff do become 'past it', arrangements are made for their early retirement. It seems therefore that many of the misfortunes of unemployment are avoidable, if employers and the employment service worked together to make them so.

In fact, whichever way you look at unemployment, bad luck for the individual seems to play at least as much a part as the actions of wider social mechanisms on groups. Even if lack of a formal job skill is not attributable to bad luck, it is bad luck if your health fails, especially in a way that affects your capacity to carry on with your work. It is bad luck if you happen to work for a firm that cannot or will not offer you a less physically demanding task. It is bad luck if your firm runs into bad times and lays off part or all of its workforce; and especially bad luck if the general demand for your own type of labour is falling off at the same time. It is the worst luck of all if these things happen when you live and have your social roots in an area where jobs are scarce and getting scarcer. Yet all these are cases where a vigorous policy could go some way towards reducing the incidence, or alleviating the consequences, of individual social misfortunes.

A changing labour market

Even in a static situation a manual worker, especially a low-status manual worker, has not only a poorly rewarded job but also poor security to keep what he has, because of the health risk attached to the job, because of the sensitivity of his trade to the consequences of failing health and because of the lack of institutional protection against dismissal. But in the current era of economic, industrial and technological change the dynamics of the situation make the position of the male manual worker even less secure. For the general direction of change is away from heavy industry, and jobs done by male manual workers, towards light industry and office and service jobs, where the good jobs require qualifications and the routine tasks are mainly performed by women. In the long term it may be impossible, and in any case undesirable, to oppose such changes, but in the short and medium term the changes are taking place more rapidly than changes in the labour force react to them. They leave male manual workers on a losing wicket; and the more narrowly we focus on particular industries, and particular parts of the country, the more severe is the problem of those found at the extreme.

Even where prosperous industries are to be found in prosperous regions – e.g. the motor industry in the Midlands – closer inspection can show that a combination of urban planning and firms' own rationalisation policies has removed manual work from the old city centres to self-contained suburban sites, taking perhaps the skilled workforce with them, but leaving the lower-status workers, the subsidiary service workers, and the dependent population high and dry. The misfortune, therefore, of being a particular type of person, at a particular place at a particular time, results for many, if not in unemployment, at least in the choice between a very poor job and tearing up all roots and starting again in a new area. The older the worker, or the lower his status, the less reasonable does the second alternative become. Either way, the change brings a considerable loss to the worker, who is sacrificed to the benefit of others. Again, consideration of the unfortunate social side-effects of macro- or micro-industrial changes does not rule such changes out of court, but it does point to the need for a greater degree of activity by government and by industry itself, to take these effects into account, to control change and to alleviate the problems caused, and draw on the resources gained through economic progress to compensate those who suffer from it.[4]

Disadvantages in employment

It is important to emphasise that inequalities in employment are not confined to wages and salaries. Throughout the following paragraphs there will be evidence to dispose of the myth of the compensatory incentive wage. This myth is based on the perfectly valid theory that, *other things being equal*, the higher wage must be paid for the job that weighs more heavily on the worker: high wages compensate for long hours, unusual time-schedules (shifts, weekends etc.), unpleasant physical working conditions, boring or positively unpleasant tasks, or some special social stigma. *Other things being equal*, this may be the case. Any particular individual may often have a choice between a pleasant lower-paid job and a less pleasant higher-paid job – the differential between skilled underground and skilled surface workers in coalmining is an example. Such compensatory differentials are perfectly fair, and constitute a greater real equality than equal wages for unequal jobs. Agreed systems of job evaluation can be used to ensure that such differentials are decided on an equitable basis.[5] Unfortunately, what may be true of the narrow range of choices open to an individual is not true in practice of the labour market as a whole, and the theory cannot be used to justify the general distribution of intrinsic and extrinsic rewards from employment – for it is clear that those who hold the trump cards win all the tricks. As we shall see, it is mainly those who earn low wages who suffer long hours, unusual time-schedules, unpleasant physical conditions, boring and unpleasant tasks and social stigmas, while it is mainly those with high salaries who experience shorter hours, regular time-schedules, pleasant conditions, interesting and pleasant tasks and social prestige.

Earnings

Low income is obviously one of the main causes (perhaps the main cause) of deprivation. It is no surprise (Table 29) to find that low wages are closely linked to low occupational status.

Table 29   Earnings of male workers, 1975[6]

	Average weekly earnings	Percentage earning less than £45 p.w.
Managerial/professional	78.2*	9*
Clerical	53.8*	34*
Skilled ⎫	59.1	18
Semi-skilled ⎬ manual	55.0	27
Unskilled ⎭	48.4	45
All non-manual	68.4	19
All manual	55.7	27

*See note 6 (2) (p.146) for detailed comment on these figures.

In general, manual workers earn less than non-manual, and for unskilled manual workers, unusually low earnings are not uncommon.

Although the figures in Table 29 are not surprising, they are by no means inevitable. In the first place, the fact that some men have no formal skill does not mean that they could not develop a skill, if a different set of conditions and opportunities were set up. In the second place, most of their jobs are probably boring and/or unpleasant, and in any case attract a degree of social stigma based on the assumption that the workers cannot achieve anything better for personal reasons. In these days of widespread education and supposedly wide-ranging opportunities it is perhaps surprising that anyone is available to perform such necessary but menial tasks without any compensation in the form of higher wages. If no one was available to do these jobs at current rates of pay, then the pay would have to go up, to persuade people to undertake them.

It is also interesting to note the severe limitations on opportunities for women, by pointing out that 79 per cent of all full-time women earn less than £45 per week and 33 per cent of them earn less than £30.[7]

Returning to the men, we can see that, in spite of the great risk of low earnings among the unskilled, not all the unskilled have poverty wages. In fact, many unskilled workers earn more than some skilled workers. The frequency of very low wages among unskilled workers can be seen in Fig. 5 from the fact that the first bar sticks out furthest

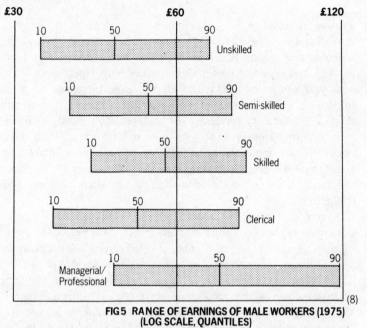

£30   £60   £120

FIG 5 RANGE OF EARNINGS OF MALE WORKERS (1975)
(LOG SCALE, QUANTILES)

to the left. The rarity of good wages is seen by the fact that the first bar sticks out least to the right. On the other hand, the range of earnings among unskilled workers is similar to, and overlaps strongly with, the ranges of semi-skilled, skilled and clerical workers. The unskilled are bottom of the league, but they are in the same league with the other types of worker, with the exception of managerial and professional workers, who are in a different and higher paid league altogether.

Level of skill alone is by no means final in determining a man's income; lack of skill has a depressing effect, but evidently geographical factors, industrial factors, overtime, trade unions and so on all have their part to play. The converse of the finding that many unskilled men are *not* in the lowest income bracket is that many skilled man *are*: indeed, there are as many skilled men earning low wages as unskilled men, in terms of actual numbers of men instead of proportions.[9] If skilled men make up as much of the total of low-wage earners as do unskilled men, low wages cannot be attributed simply to the low skills of the latter. Evidently other factors, many of which may come under our general heading of luck, have an important part to play.

Prospective earnings

A worker's earnings need to be assessed not only in terms of the spending power they give him this week, but also in terms of the earnings and spending power he can confidently expect next week, next year and in the next ten or twenty years. In general the ideal might be a stable income, in the sense that it does not go up and down unpredictably, combined with a foreseeable steady increase, in real terms, from year to year over one's lifetime. Both these conditions are more nearly fulfilled for non-manual workers than for manual workers. In neither case does there seem to be much difference between levels of worker within each of these two categories.

Firstly, how steady are incomes? Of course, the general picture for both manual and non-manual workers is of a small but steady rise in monetary incomes, first to counteract rising prices, and secondly (at least in the past) as a result of real increases in the level of prosperity. Discounting this general trend, however, and looking at changing relative incomes within each group, the picture is rather different. If the earnings of the same workers are measured in one week in April in two consecutive years, less than half the manual workers can be said to have earned 'about the average' increase (the average increase ±100%). About one-third have increased their earnings by more than twice the average, while nearly a quarter are earning less than the year before. On the other hand, three-quarters of non-manual workers are 'normal' in their increases, one-sixth having had a big rise and only one in ten having experienced a drop in earnings.[10]

Thus, although some manual workers received surprisingly high increases, others, equally surprisingly, lost ground. In fact, at first sight, the pattern of changes seems rather equitable – those with exceptionally low earnings often got exceptional increases, while top earners fell back. Unfortunately, the tendency of the extremes to close in on the centre is neatly balanced by a tendency for the centre to spread out to the extremes – average manual workers (last year) tend to be above or below average at the next stage.

If we used a manual worker's last year's earnings to try to help us predict this year's, the result would be about *twice* as accurate as if we had just guessed he would earn the general average. But if we used a non-manual worker's past to predict his future, the result would be *four* times as accurate. For the workers themselves (although they will not think so mathematically) a non-manual worker can be twice as confident about the future as a manual worker.[11] And confidence about future earnings is vital to proper budgeting.

These figures are based on a comparison between one week (or month) in 1971 and the same week (or month) in 1972, and they therefore cannot sort out variations between weeks from variations between years, though seasonal fluctuation was virtually eliminated, as both surveys were done in April. It is known, of course, that manual workers are subject to weekly or monthly variation, according to the amount of overtime they work, while non-manual workers, who rarely do overtime, lack this source of variation. This factor seems to account for about half the difference in consistency between the two types of worker.[12] The rest of the difference must be either through variations in bonus payments etc., or through different success in negotiating increases for different manual trades or industries, or through individuals rising or falling in their local league table. In 1975 only 74 per cent of the average manual worker's earnings was provided by basic wages. The rest came from overtime (14 per cent), shift premiums etc. (3 per cent), payment by results (9 per cent). For non-manual workers 94 per cent came from basic pay.[13]

Thus non-manual workers looking to the future can be more certain that their progress will be similar to that of their peers than manual workers can. The second question is what that average future progress looks like. It is well known that the institutional career structure for the two groups is different – that manual workers simply look forward to continuing in their current job, and hope for increased prosperity through progress of their group as a whole, while non-manual workers, particularly those in the managerial and professional streams, can expect promotion and also an annual increment within their present grade (Table 30).

Table 30   Mean earnings by age. Male manual and non-manual workers (1975)[14]

Age	Manual	Non-manual
18-20	£40	(£33)*
21-24	£51	£46
25-29	£56	£60
30-39	£59	£72
40-49	£58	£77
50-59	£55	£73
60-64	£51	(£63)*

*The figures for non-manual workers aged 18-20 and 60-64 are artificially low, as most senior (higher-paid) non-manual workers' careers last only from 21 to 60.

In the abstract it seems far better to look forward like a non-manual worker to a continuously increasing absolute and relative standard of living, as present difficulties are most easily borne if the end is in sight. There may also be practical advantages – for instance, in negotiating a mortgage. On the other hand, the pattern of manual workers' wages may not be wholly a disadvantage for them. First, if manual workers' limited lifetime earnings were tipped heavily against youth and in favour of age, this would leave them very poor indeed during their early years. Secondly, if that occurred, the low wages would come at precisely the time when need for income is greatest, while there are dependent children to be fed and clothed. Thirdly, manual workers can look forward to an increased income when their children grow up and their wives are released for work. Perhaps the steady growth of non-manual incomes is an advantage for non-manual people (and especially for their wives, who need never work), but the converse may not be much of a disadvantage for manual workers and their families.

Hours of work

No prizes are offered for guessing which types of worker suffer the longest hours (Table 31).

Table 31 Total weekly hours of work for different occupational groups[15]

	Manual (per cent)	Non-manual (per cent)
Over 36 hours	99	78
Over 42 hours	54	15
Over 48 hours	27	5
Over 54 hours	12	3
Over 60 hours	5	1

Although 42 hours of work may not seem excessive, over half of all full-time manual workers do more than that. Over a quarter of them do more than the equivalent of 8 hours a day, 6 days a week. Six 10-hour days, or seven 8½-hour days seem excessive by any standard, yet one in twenty manual workers suffers more than that – an undoubted deprivation both for themselves and for their families. Nor are they getting rich in the process – the average earnings for a 60- to 70-hour week (in 1974) were £1 less than the average earnings for a 35-hour week.[16] This is because the 60- to 70-hour weeks are almost all worked by manual workers and the 35-hour weeks by non-manual, often senior, workers.

In the case of hours and overtime there is little difference among manual workers according to skill level. In fact, part of the explanation for the fact that some unskilled workers earn more than some skilled workers lies in variations in the amount of overtime available.

In addition to long hours, manual workers are liable to work inconvenient hours, either as a condition of service or in order to maintain their earnings. In 1974 20 per cent of manual workers received a 'shift or other premium payment', compared with 4 per cent of non-manual workers.[17]. (The 20 per cent represents a minimum estimate of those affected, as some jobs, e.g. cinema operator, or night driver, may entail unusual hours with the premium assumed within the basic wages.) Shifts, especially night shifts, are not merely inconvenient; they are often exhausting and disturbing to both worker and family.

The job itself

Although some non-manual tasks may be intrinsically unpleasant, and some manual tasks may be intrinsically pleasant, there can be little doubt that in general the balance is tipped the other way. Manual jobs are the more likely to entail unpleasant work. Whatever way in which work can be unpleasant, the principal examples are to be found low in the occupational scale: jobs here may demand heavy physical labour; be routine and boring; allow little or no scope for the individual to determine what he should do, or how or when he should do it; have to be performed in conditions of extreme heat or cold, or extreme noise or smell; or bring with them a high risk of physical accident or long-term ill-health. All these conditions are associated with low status and low pay. While many of them may provide slightly higher pay for the individual than any alternative, pleasanter, job that individual might consider, it is here that the idea of high incomes providing compensation for unpleasant tasks falls down. Thus, a recent PEP survey that asked workers to evaluate particular aspects of their jobs showed that the lower the occupational status, the greater the dissatisfaction (Table 32).

On this basis senior non-manual workers have the best of everything in their jobs, and semi-skilled or unskilled workers have the worst of it. Clearly among the latter group will be found most of those with jobs not just 'poor' but 'bad'; they can be said to be suffering severe deprivation on the job, as well as in the monetary rewards they receive for it.

It has sometimes been found that when workers are asked to give a

Table 32 Attitudes of male workers to aspects of their jobs [18]

	Managerial/ professional (per cent)	Clerical (per cent)	Skilled manual (per cent)	Semi/ unskilled (per cent)
There is 'no scope' to influence decisions affecting the work	17	23	43	63
Promotion is 'not at all' likely	17	13	30	43
The work is 'sometimes' or 'often' boring	23	38	51	57
The worker does not deem his place 'very' secure	29	41	56	61

general assessment of how satisfied they are with their job, there is not much variation between occupational groups, and that such small variation as does exist does not follow the predictable pattern shown above.[19] Since variation in assessment of the particulars does, in fact, exist, the apparent uniformity of the answers to the general question (in which nearly nine out of ten workers declare themselves to be satisfied, and around a half 'very' satisfied) suggests that this general evaluation is in relation to the job market in which the worker finds himself. This only reinforces the suggestion that inequality is founded on limitations in opportunity. We know for a fact that there are many jobs that are better in every sense of the word than those currently held by unskilled or semi-skilled manual workers. Those workers know it too. But they also know that those better jobs are not for them. They have taken a job that is the best for them within the narrow range available to them. They, like other people, express their satisfaction within the terms of the possible. They are satisfied that they are right to retain their present job, because it is the best they can get. If the unskilled are satisfied, it is because they are pleased to have a job at all. The answers to a further question in the same survey support this (Table 33).

Table 33 Chances of finding another satisfactory job if worker lost this one [20]

	Managerial/ professional (per cent)	Clerical (per cent)	Skilled (per cent)	Semi/ unskilled (per cent)
Very difficult	28	27	30	41
Fairly difficult / Not sure / Not very difficult	50	59	55	52
Not at all difficult	21	16	15	7
'Very difficult' minus 'not at all difficult'	(7)	(11)	(15)	(34)

One hole has to be all right, if you can't see a better one.

Terms of employment

In one major way, and in many minor ways, variations in terms of employment repeat the now familiar picture. First, non-manual workers, especially those in the senior career streams, are much more secure in their jobs than manual workers, especially the unskilled. There is a statutory minimum period of notice that varies, according to length of service, from one week to four weeks. Only 13 per cent of manufacturing employers claim to be more generous than this to their 'operatives'; between 26 per cent and 29 per cent are more generous to foremen, clerical workers and technicians; 53 per cent are more generous to their middle managers; and 61 per cent to their senior managers.[21] Within the 'operative' class we should expect the un-skilled to be least likely to receive above-minimum treatment; more-over, many of them, being casuals or recently employed, would not benefit even from the legal requirements. Thirdly, an employer's abil-ity to 'lay off' production workers during slack periods, often with-out a guaranteed wage, further undermines manual workers' security.

The consequences of these differences in job security may seem slight in a day-to-day view of employment, since most people rarely face the sack. When the crunch comes, however, the consequences are enormous. In the first place, a long period of notice is one of many reasons why senior staff are unlikely to be sacked at all, since redundancies would have to be planned well in advance, and dismissals following a personal altercation can be reconsidered after tempers have cooled. Secondly, once a man has been sacked, a long period of notice means not only that he has time to seek a new job, but also that he does not have to weaken his bargaining position by confessing to prospective employers that he is unemployed. So, to those affected, actual variations in length of notice (Table 34) are extremely important.

Table 34 Length of (informal) notice received by the unemployed, of various occupational status[22]

	Man./ Prof. (per cent)	Clerical (per cent)	Skilled manual (per cent)	Semi-skilled (per cent)	Un-skilled (per cent)
1 week or less	12	28	42	51	54
Over 1 week to 1 month	15	20	22	25	25
Over 1 month to 3 months	19	24	17	9	7
Over 3 months	50	27	15	13	9
(Can't remember)	(5)	(2)	(3)	(3)	(5)

Other variations in terms of employment may seem of less importance, in that they have no great practical effect on the majority of employees of any class. On the other hand, if deprivations are to be seen as social accidents, manual workers are obviously worse protected than non-manual against the short- or long-term consequences of such accidents.

Thus, although manual workers are more likely to have to take time off work for sickness than non-manual, only half of them receive sick pay, compared with three-quarters of junior non-manual workers and nearly all professional and managerial workers.[23] So too, more than five employers in six will allow time off with pay for domestic reasons (wife sick etc.) to non-manual workers, but less than one in three allow the same licence to manual workers.[24]

Finally, nearly all manual workers have to clock-on to record their attendance at work; nearly all lose pay if they are late; and nearly all will be sacked if they are regularly absent without leave. In contrast, hardly any managers clock-on; hardly any are subject to pay deductions if late; and one-third of them would not be sacked for persistent absenteeism, even if it was noticed.[25]

So the disadvantages in employment arising out of a man's opportunities being limited to manual work are several; and if the limitation is to unskilled work, the disadvantages are even greater. The list of disadvantages has been confined to aspects of employment where manual workers are recognisably worse off; it could be extended with a list of differences between manual and non-manual workers – separate canteen facilities, different times of starting work, different payment mechanisms, even different toilet facilities – where manual workers are not necessarily worse off, and where the only purpose of the distinction appears to be to maintain the unbridgeability of the gulf between workers of different status.

This book is mainly about 'deprivation', and deprivation has, in other chapters, been understood to refer to problems experienced by a minority of the people, whose standard of life in one dimension or another is unacceptably below the normal standards of the rest of society. Yet in this chapter the focus has been mainly on a distinction between manual workers and non-manual workers, even though unskilled workers have received extra attention. How is it possible to discuss a group of workers who make up well over half of the workforce as though they were deprived? The answer is that, although the current situation of the majority of manual workers cannot, by definition, be considered a deprivation (more a lack of privilege), the seeds of deprivation are to be found in a manual occupation. If most manual workers receive a wage reasonably close to the average, it is nevertheless manual workers and especially the unskilled who risk having a very low wage now, or who cannot be confident for their future wages. If most manual workers work around 42 hours a week, it is manual workers who risk having to work 60 hours a week. If most manual workers have average working conditions, it is manual workers who may have to suffer atrocious conditions. If most manual workers have steady jobs, it is nevertheless manual workers who are most likely to be sacked, and who will suffer the heaviest consequences if they are. If manual work does not itself constitute deprivation, it is in manual work that the potential for deprivation is to be found.

Disadvantages following employment

This conclusion is heavily reinforced when we consider inequalities in the external consequences of work. In a later chapter it will be shown how manual workers, especially the unskilled, are highly likely to experience chronic illness or early death. Part of the explanation for that must lie in the nature and/or conditions of the work itself. Earlier in this chapter it was shown how manual workers, especially the unskilled, were highly likely to experience a period of unemployment. But the most serious consequence of low-status employment comes after working life is over, during retirement; for, however deprivation is defined, it is impossible to escape the conclusion that most working-class pensioners are deprived. As far as their income is concerned, it is in their working life that the origin of their deprivation is to be found; and this will continue as long as the national guaranteed pension arrangements fall so far short of the earnings of those who remain in work.

It is surprisingly difficult to find clear figures on the distribution of occupational pensions, but what figures there are suggest that most non-manual workers are members of schemes, but only about half the manual workers are. Almost certainly the range of inequality is greater if the two broad groups are divided into the five narrower categories used elsewhere. Moreover, many of the pension schemes to which manual workers do belong pay very small amounts, with no allowance for inflation. As a result, the great majority of working-class pensioners depend on the state pension, and are in undoubted poverty, at a period in their life when their many other troubles may make poverty most difficult to bear.

One reaction to these facts is to argue for the spread of occupational pension schemes down the social scale until we approach a situation in which all employers offer pensions to all their employees. Second thoughts, however, suggest that such progress would not make pensioners much better off and might even have a harmful effect.

First, the pitifully small income to be derived from most occupational pensions means that they may make little difference to the pensioners' prosperity. In 1971 30 per cent of married couples and 40 per cent of single old people in receipt of pensions received less than £2 per week. Among single women (many of them widows) nearly a quarter got less than £1.[26] Even these sums might be of some use, but those without any occupational pension at all might be just as well off relying on the provision of state Supplementary Pensions. Thus, for many former manual workers and their widows, the occupational pension must make little difference, or no difference at all. Annuities and occupational pensions contribute a mere 16 per cent of the total income available to old couples, 20 per cent to single old men and 10 per cent to single old women. Single old women form about one-tenth of all households in this country: in 1974, the average non-state pensions for them was £1.75 per week.[27] A high proportion of these average figures must be attributable to the satisfactory pensions secured by senior non-manual workers, leaving most of the rest with nothing at all.

Secondly, it seems impossible that occupational pensions can ever provide equitably for all old people. Those who spend many of their 'working' years out of work through sickness or disablement cannot be covered. Those (especially unskilled workers) who for one reason or another have to change jobs frequently will have little or no cover. Women workers and widows are actually a greater risk (as they live longer than men) and therefore can count on only a small pension. There will always be some people who will have to depend on the state pension, but the fewer of them there are, the greater will be their social isolation, even assuming that the state pension retains its present relative value. And the fewer of them there are, the less will be the political pressure to treat them generously, and the greater will be the tendency to abandon them to their fate as having failed to take precautions for their old age.

Thirdly, because most occupational pension schemes place a premium on long-term employment in one job, the current system constitutes a deterrent to labour mobility, especially for middle-aged workers, for whom, as we have seen, remaining in an old-fashioned job brings lower earnings.

Thus, although occupational pension schemes were desirable and necessary in the days before the state accepted any responsibility for the income of the elderly, they can now be seen to be ineffective in increasing most old people's welfare, to be a hindrance to the state's accepting a greater and more generous responsibility, and to be a (possibly minor) obstacle to the social and economic benefits of greater labour mobility.

Limited access

All the analysis so far in this chapter points to the same conclusion: that (although in some respects a clerical job is no better than a skilled manual job) it is manual workers who suffer disadvantage in their employment, and it is manual workers who carry the risk of severe deprivation as a consequence of their employment. This, of course, is not a new or a surprising conclusion. The general inequality between the broad groups has always been well known, even if there has been from time to time, as at present, a feeling among some members of the non-manual group that some types of manual worker are doing exceptionally well. The important point, for this study, is that the incidence of deprivation seems to stem from the more general inequality rather than from some peculiarity of the deprived.

There remains a further important question. We live in a society in which, unlike, say, feudal Europe or apartheid South Africa, there are no agreed overt controls over who should be entitled to jobs of various rewards and status. If non-manual jobs, particularly mana-gerial and professional jobs, are so much more attractive in so many ways than the manual jobs held by the majority of the workforce, why do not manual workers seek and obtain these better jobs? After all, it is on the basis of 'incentive' that the existence of these better rewarded jobs is justified.* If a proportion of the present manual

---

*Economists would justify higher rewards in terms of the 'market', not incentives. But high prices in a market are based on incentives anyway – a rise in the price of butter is an incentive to produce more of it.

workforce succeeded in crossing the great divide, not only would they themselves be better off, but also, by increasing the competition for the better jobs, and reducing the supply of people willing to work at manual tasks, they ought to bring about a reduction in the 'price differential' within the labour market.

One possible answer to this question is that those who remain in manual occupations are not willing and/or not able to undertake the role at present filled by non-manual and particularly senior non-manual workers. If that provided anywhere near a full explanation, the present inequality in reward (if not the inequality in job security and pensions) would be justified. If, on the other hand, the answer was that manual workers are prevented from taking non-manual or senior jobs, then the differential would be shown to be artificial, unjustified, and, indeed, inefficient.

Some commentators appear to adopt the first view: that the differential must be just, because, in our free and fair society, anyone can seek any job. A few commentators appear, at least for the sake of argument, to believe that the differential is totally unjust, because it is impossible for a working-class person to aspire to other than a working-class job. Most of us, however, will not adopt either of these extreme positions: it is possible for some members of manual working-class families to get to the top, but there are a number of difficulties that stand in their way. The logical conclusion of such an intermediate position is that, while some differentials between the rewards and statuses of different jobs are just and functionally necessary, the current width of those differentials could and should be reduced somewhat for each of the hindrances to occupational mobility that could and should be eliminated.

It is well beyond the scope of the present study to describe, let alone measure, all the possible hindrances which appear to exist, and the complex set of interactions between them. Nevertheless, it is clear from various surveys of the relation between fathers' and sons' occupational statuses that it is by no means easy for the son of a working-class father to reach middle-class, much less upper middle-class, status. It is difficult to quote statistics, because methodological differences between surveys of the relationship lead to apparent differences in the findings.[28] They all agree, however, that, although it is not possible to predict a son's status with much accuracy, there is a strong tendency for non-manual workers to have had non-manual fathers, and for manual workers to have had manual fathers.

Moreover, *within the non-manual group*, there is a similarly strong distinction between clerical and managerial or professional occupations; but within the manual group there is a relatively weak link between fathers and sons in terms of skill level. (There is a widely held belief that it is relatively easy to transfer from clerical to senior non-manual position: it is easy only relative to the chances of manual workers. It also indicates a possible reason why clerical workers are not much better off than manual workers.)

The reasons for this restriction in occupational mobility must be diffuse. It is partly a matter of educational qualifications; but then, nearly a third of all manual workers have recognised qualifications, and over a third of non-manual workers do not. It may be partly as a result of differences in the cultural and material environments of upbringing; partly a result of an educational system that devotes too much of its attention to distinguishing between the able and the less able, and not enough on trying to lessen the gap; partly a matter of family influence;* partly a consequence of hurdles deliberately set up by 'the professions' to limit the numbers in their field; partly social class discrimination achieved subconsciously in much the same way as racial discrimination; partly a question of working-class young men accepting working-class status instead of making an assault on the hurdles that they may see before them; and partly a matter of the occupational opportunities existing in a particular place, at a particular time, for people whose immediate needs prevent a wider, longer search for something better. Add up all these partial reasons and we might achieve something of the full explanation.

Thus inequality of career opportunity, which prevents a large proportion of the workforce from reacting to incentives, seems to be largely instrumental in maintaining the degree of inequality of status and rewards. A second contribution may also stem from differences between the opportunities within each stratum. If managerial and professional workers are relatively free to move from job to job in a healthy free market, in response to changing social and economic demands, they will, as a group, fare better than manual workers, if the latter are restricted by the structure of the housing and employment markets from escaping from jobs of declining value, and taking advantage of new opportunities. Active labour market policies, while they might have little direct effect on mobility between manual and

*According to one survey, 83 per cent of managing directors have managerial or professional fathers.[29]

non-manual, ought nevertheless to bestow both social and economic
advantages on the members of each group.

NOTES

1 See W. W. Daniel, *A National Survey of the Unemployed*, PEP
  Broadsheet No. 546, 1974.
2 Census 1971.
3 See S. Mukherjee, *Through No Fault of Their Own*, PEP/Mac-
  donald, 1973.
4 The various problems limiting the middle-aged manual worker's
  search for a new job in the face of change have been reviewed in
  R. Berthoud, 'Employment in a changing Labour Market', paper
  presented to Centre for Environmental Studies seminar on
  Employment in the Inner City (1975).
5 See W. W. Daniel and N. McIntosh, *The Right to Manage?*,
  PEP/Macdonald, 1972.
6 Dept. of Employment, *New Earnings Survey 1975*, H.M.S.O.,
  1975. There are two unsatisfactory features about the summary
  table presented in the text:
  (1) The distinction within *manual* employees between skilled,
      semi-skilled and unskilled is no longer shown by the *N.E.S.*
      For the purpose of Table 29 and Fig. 5, it has been assumed
      that the distribution of wages by skill level within manual
      workers was the same in 1974 as it was in 1972 (the last year
      when the *N.E.S.* analysed by skill level).
  (2) The distinction within *non-manual* employees between man-
      agerial/professional and clerical workers is derived from the
      N.E.S. on the basis that occupations I to VI are managerial/
      professional and occupations VII to IX are clerical. Unfortu-
      nately, this appears to place 'intermediate' non-manual work-
      ers in the senior category, whereas in other analyses in this
      book they have been placed in the junior category. The effect
      of this misplacement is to make the managerial/professional
      category too close to the non-manual average, and the clerical
      category too far away. Estimated true figures, correcting for
      the misplacement are as follows:

| | Average earnings | | Proportion below £45 | |
	Apparent	True	Apparent (per cent)	True (per cent)
Managerial/ professional	£78.2	£81.5	9	7
Other non-manual	£53.8	£57.7	34	25

Even after correction, of course, clerical workers' salaries are lower than the wages of skilled manual workers. This is out of line with other comparisons between these two groups, perhaps because male clerical workers are in direct competition with the large supply of female clerical labour, at very low pay. This possibility is supported by the fact that the occupations with the lowest male premium are those in which women outnumber the men – clerical etc., and catering, cleaning etc.

7 *Ibid.*

8 See note 6 above. Fig. 5 uses a log. scale. This relates distances not to absolute amounts in £s but to ratios between amounts. Thus the gap between £60 and £30 is the same as the gap between £120 and £60. In effect, the chart gives importance to *how many times as much* one man earns as another, not *how much more*.

The left-hand end of each bar represents the weekly wage *below* which the *lowest 10 per cent* of the members of the group fall. The right-hand end of the bar represents the weekly wage above which the *highest 10 per cent* of the members of the group rise. Each bar effectively gives the range of earnings of members of the group, excluding high and low extremes. The vertical stroke gives the median – the wage dividing the top half from the bottom half.

9 In the *New Earnings Survey 1972* 40.8 per cent of the 7,588 unskilled men in the sample (3,097 men) earned less than £25; and 14.0 per cent of the 21,804 skilled men in the sample (3,053 men) earned less than £25.

10 Department of Employment, *New Earnings Survey 1972* (Annex), H.M.S.O., 1973.

11 *Ibid.* The correlation coefficient between 1971 and 1972 for manual workers (weekly earnings including overtime) is 0.682, meaning 46.5 per cent of the variance is explained, leaving half unexplained. For non-manual workers the coefficient is 0.871; 75.9 per cent explained and a quarter unexplained.

12 *Ibid.* The correlation coefficients discounting overtime are 0.785 (manual) and 0.882 (non-manual).

13 *New Earnings Survey 1975.*
14 *Ibid.*
15 *Ibid.*
16 *New Earnings Survey 1974.*
17 *New Earnings Survey 1975.*
18 Data from survey reported in W.W. Daniel, *The PEP Survey on Inflation*, PEP Broadsheet No. 553, 1975.
19 For instance, *General Household Survey, op. cit.*
20 See note 18.
21 D. Wedderburn and C. Craig, 'Relative Deprivation in Work', in D. Wedderburn (ed.), *Poverty, Inequality and Class Structure*, Cambridge U.P., 1974.
22 W.W. Daniel, *A National Survey of the Unemployed, op. cit.*
23 O.P.C.S., *General Household Survey, op. cit.*
24 D. Wedderburn and C. Craig, *op. cit.*
25 *Ibid.*
26 Central Statistical Office, *Social Trends, No. 4*, H.M.S.O., 1973, 'The Elderly'.
27 Department of Employment, *Family Expenditure Survey 1974*, H.M.S.O.
28 The author has compared analyses of the father-son relationship from four different sources: (1) D.V. Glass, *Social Mobility in Britain*, Routledge & Kegan Paul, 1954; (2) K. Hope, *Trends in the Openness of British Society*, Nuffield College, Oxford, Mimeo, 1974; (3) O.P.C.S., *General Household Survey 1971, op. cit.*, based on hitherto unpublished data; and (4) unpublished data from the PEP survey reported in W.W. Daniel, *The PEP Survey on Inflation, op.cit.*

No two of these analyses tell exactly the same story. Part of the differences can be assumed to derive from differences in the classification of occupations, but part remain unexplained. The *G.H.S.* data can be used as an example, in a simplified form. In a sample of 1,000 there would be the following combinations:

SON	FATHER Man./ prof.	Other non-manual	Skilled manual	Semi/unskilled manual
Man./prof.	73	30		
	[174]		[215]	
Other non-manual	35	36		
Skilled manual			208	138
Semi/unskilled manual	[101]		[510]	
			75	89

From these figures we can deduce a measure of the consistency of father-son relationship. The first considers manual versus non-manual (using the boxed figures); the second considers man./prof. versus other non-manual, using only those cases where both father and son were non-manual (the non-boxed figures in the top left quadrant); and the third, similarly within manual (bottom right quadrant). The measure used is:

$$\frac{(O-E)\times 100}{(N-E)}$$

where 'O' is the observed number of sons who remained in the same group as their father; 'E' is the expected number, on the assumption of no relationship; 'N' is the total sample.

The measure, which ranges from 0 to 100, can be interpreted as the proportion of sons who 'should' have changed group, who did not in fact do so.

Between manual and non-manual	30
Within non-manual	22
Within manual	13

Equivalent figures from the other three surveys are:

	Glass	Hope	Daniel	Average of all four
Between manual and non-manual	32	29	41	33
Within non-manual	45	24	30	30¼
Within manual	19	13	14	14¾

All the figures agree that mobility from class to class is possible, but that the chances of the son of a manual worker crossing both hurdles up to managerial/professional status are much less than they 'ought' to be.

29 M. Young and P. Willmott, *The Symmetrical Family*, Routledge & Kegan Paul, 1973.

6 The Geography of Poverty

If poverty is a name for the unfortunate end of inequality, and if people should be described as deprived in comparison with others, then it is important that we should discuss the basis for comparison. Clearly Britain is not deprived at all viewed from United Nations headquarters; on the other hand, observers in Washington, Stockholm or even Brussels may well see us as a deprived nation. Even within one country the perspective is important: within Britain the North West region may be seen to be in trouble; within the North West Liverpool, say, might be noted; within Liverpool the district of Vauxhall has been singled out for attention; and no doubt Vauxhall has its streets and households that are worse off than others.

The existence of regions, towns and districts that are worse off than others is well known, and has been the subject of much discussion and some policy in recent years. Indeed, it sometimes seems that multiple deprivation of *places* has somewhat overshadowed multiple deprivation of *people* as a subject for concern. It is, of course, reasonable to assume that deprived localities contain deprived people, and that alleviation of problems affecting an area will have a beneficial effect on its inhabitants. There are a number of reasons why this angle of approach is attractive.

1 A deprived area is fairly easily visible to the naked eye: old and decrepit housing, poor public amenities, evidence of local vandalism and so on. Such areas afflict the public conscience; it is evident that many problems exist in the area, and there is an immediate call for action.
2 There are administrative, even conceptual, advantages in deciding on a concentrated action programme to solve the problems of a particular locality.
3 Many of the problems of such places are intrinsically problems of

150

the area, imposed on the individuals who happen to live there. Environmental problems are the most obvious examples.
4 Similarly, many of the problems, including, for instance, education, as well as the environment, can make use of area-based action, as well as action aimed specifically at individuals. New schools, new parks, rerouting of heavy traffic, help *all* the people in the area affected, not just the worst off, so that it is correct to take such action where the greatest number of sufferers is to be found.
5 If deprived individuals or households are indeed heavily concentrated into particular localities, then solving most of the problems in such areas will help most of the deprived people.

It is therefore useful to look at the problem from a geographical perspective, not only because an individual situation needs to be seen in its locational context, but because an areal analysis may lead to a number of conclusions about causes and possible solutions. It is worth bearing in mind, however, that social geography has none of the inevitability of physical geography. Whatever the influence of geographical factors, they will never give the whole explanation of deprivation, nor will they indicate the whole solution. Indeed, even if they give much of the explanation, they do not necessarily suggest much of a solution. These are points that will be discussed at the end of the chapter, after the nature of the geographical factors has been considered.

Variations between regions

It is well known that there are wide variations in the country's prosperity on the largest scale – at regional level. There is an abundance of information available to support this conclusion, even though the grain of the available data – regions, or at best counties – has so far been too coarse for any precise mapping of economic contours.[1]

It is, nevertheless, possible to observe differences which suggest that it is not always appropriate to consider the country as a single unit for administrative or economic purposes. Generally speaking, London, or at least the area immediately surrounding it, is prosperous, becoming more prosperous, and attracting migrant population both from the Commonwealth and from the rest of the country. This region of prosperity spreads north-westwards to the West Midlands.

Meanwhile, Lancashire, at the other end of the industrial axis that had built up by the beginning of the century, is at best stagnant, or even in decline, together with the old industrial areas in Yorkshire, South Wales, the North East and Central Scotland. And there are huge areas in East Anglia, the South West, Wales, the North, Scotland and Northern Ireland, which never obtained the full benefits (or, for that matter, some of the problems) of the old growth in manufacturing, nor of the new growth in office and service employment. They seem condemned to a perpetual struggle to keep up. (North Sea oil may, of course, help Scotland and the North East in future.)

This is, of course, far too simple a picture of an enormously complicated subject. But it seems to be a fair summary, whether one considers incomes, or social security, or employment, or migration, or health or whatever. The major points that need clarifying are, first, whether London itself should be considered as part of the South Eastern growth area, or whether it is more akin to the older industrial areas to the North; and, secondly, whether the problems are more acute in the stagnant or declining industrial areas, or in the never-made-it rural areas.

One common suggestion is that regional inequalities would be partly eliminated if there were more regional self-determination and self-government to counteract the gravitational pull of London. That might help. On the other hand, if we look at variations between towns and counties, which in some fields have local autonomy, there is not much evidence of uniformity.

Variations between towns

Of course, different towns (and villages) are more and less prosperous than others: generally the least prosperous towns can be expected to be found in the least prosperous regions, but local factors cause considerable differences among the towns in each region or sub-region.[2] Local variations in prosperity are a feature of economic and social geography similar in kind to regional variations. It follows that some local authorities have far more economic and social problems than others, and far more deprivation to deal with. It may be that some of the towns with the most deprivation are also towns with a low average rateable value, and thus with a poor source of income. But it has been clear for a long time that variations among local authorities in their given circumstances are very slight compared with the unaccountable variations in the services provided by the council to its citizens, in schooling, in social services, in local health services and so on. The extent of these variations has been pointed out repeatedly;[3] Table 35 shows one recently reported example.

Table 35   Expenditure per 1,000 population under 18 years
on preventing children being taken into care, 1971-2[4]

	County boroughs		London boroughs		County councils	
Spending nothing	Tynemouth		Bexley		Montgomery	
	Preston		Wandsworth		Cardigan	
	York					
	Oldham					
	Birkenhead					
Lowest three	Merthyr		Redbridge	£23	Stafford	£4.07
	Tydfil	£4	Harrow	£15	Essex	£2.69
	Sunderland	£3	Hillingdon	£6	E. Riding	£1.68
	Kingston upon					
	Hull	£1				
Highest three	Oxford	£572	Lambeth	£2,294	Kent	£216
	Rochdale	£512	Islington	£1,383	Wiltshire	£171
	Bath	£215	Westminster	£1,010	Huntingdon-	
					shire	£91

If local control over services is desirable on grounds other than of historical continuity, then it is because local services should be tailored to local needs and local priorities. But low spenders can scarcely justify their inactivity in terms of lack of need for a service. On *a priori* grounds it is scarcely conceivable that need should vary so widely among counties or among towns as do these variations in expenditure. Two careful attempts to find some relation between need and expenditure, by analysis of financial and social data, have failed to produce any logical association.[5] Nor can we believe that local priorities can provide the explanation. Are the people of Oxford 572 times as concerned about child care as the people of Kingston upon Hull? Or are the people of Kent eighty times as concerned as the people of Essex, on the other side of the Thames estuary? We can only conclude that levels of service are largely determined by the caprice of the local authority. That is fine for people benefiting from capriciously generous services, but rather unfortunate for those suffering from capricious stinginess.[6] Local democracy seems to need a rather better level of central supervision, to iron out some of the gross inequalities among areas.

Not that central control automatically eliminates such discrepancies, for they exist too in services with a national network. The Health Service provides plenty of evidence of variations in service, usually tending to favour the south at the expense of the north in personnel and facilities.[7] No one seems to know why there are 74 per cent more beds per head of population in the S.W. Metropolitan hospital region than in the Sheffield hospital region (Table 36).

Table 36   Allocated beds per 1,000 population, in English hospital regions, 1972[8]

S.W. Metropolitan	12.9	N.E. Metropolitan	8.7
Liverpool	10.1	Manchester	8.6
South Western	10.0	Wessex	8.1
Leeds	9.8	Birmingham	8.0
N.W. Metropolitan	9.5	East Anglia	7.8
Newcastle	9.2	Oxford	7.7
S.E. Metropolitan	8.9	Sheffield	7.4

These variations cannot be explained in terms of differences in need, nor in differences of medical practice. There seems no reason at all why Sheffield should have only three-quarters the service of next-door Leeds.

So the hospital service, which is administered regionally but controlled centrally, also shows wide variations; and there are, no doubt, individual towns that gain or lose from a decision on the siting of a particular hospital. Nevertheless, the administrative framework is available to work for greater equality, even if it is not used to that end. The possibility is demonstrated by the policy known (rather infelicitously) as 'negative direction', whereby G.P.s are encouraged to practise in less popular areas.

So far we have been considering differences on a fairly large geographical scale. Although different regions or sub-regions have common boundaries, they are effectively in separate places. They may be different in their physical geography – in geology, topography, climate, access to transport networks, and so on. Since they are physically separated from each other by distance, which requires expenditure of time and money to traverse, they are bound to develop a certain independence of each other, which would partially explain some of the development and perpetuation of social and economic differences.

Theoretically, the existence of physical distance as a social barrier can be used to discount some of the worst social effects of geographical inequality. The theory of relative deprivation (see p. 27) emphasises the importance of an individual's *reference groups* in determining his perception of deprivation. Since reference groups are likely to be formed from among those with whom the individual is in social-or at least visual-contact, it can be suggested that if people are going to be poor, or badly housed, or whatever, they will feel less deprived if they are surrounded by others who are in a similar position, and if there is a comparative absence of those who are more prosperous. Thus regional inequality may damp the effect of a given degree of general inequality. Of course, this does not justify regional inequality; moreover, increasing mobility and the mass media will tend to encourage the formation of national, as well as local, reference groups.

The other side of the coin also needs stressing-that those who are poor, or nearly poor, in prosperous areas will suffer relative deprivation more acutely. This is a particularly important point when we consider the existence of deprivation within the more prosperous cities.

Variations within towns

Like so many of the aspects of inequality that have recently become the subject of public concern, the fact that rich and poor are not randomly distributed across the urban landscape is neither a new phenomenon nor a new discovery. There have been rich quarters and poor quarters probably ever since cities were first developed, although the pattern has varied. Perhaps one could generalise by saying that where a city's main function is commercial and/or administrative, the rich occupy the centre, as is still partly true in some of the most favoured parts of London today, whereas primarily industrial cities have held the workers in the centre while the wealthy lived outside-as observed by Engels in Manchester, and still observable today.

Although the concentration of deprived people in deprived areas within towns is so well known as to have become one of the clichés of current debate, there are a number of important questions, the answers to which are not understood or have sometimes simply been assumed. How great is this concentration? Is it a single phenomenon with simple implications, or does it consist of a network of phenomena with only the geographical factor as a common thread? Does the concentration of various problems into certain areas imply a concentration of problems in certain families or individuals? Does the concentration play a functional role in depressing the life chances of these individuals in a vicious circle, or is concentration simply an observation that people who would anyway be poor tend to live next door to each other? Whichever the answer to the previous question, does concentration offer the opportunity for area-based social policy that would reduce the extent of deprivation for the residents? Would such policy be palliative or curative? If such areas were eliminated or prevented from developing, what would the consequences be, either for the generality of their present residents or for particular types of people?

It will be clear that the subject is immensely complicated. And much of the discussion, much of the policy, even much of the research on the subject will be admitted to assume answers to some of these fundamental questions that have not been tested. Perhaps that is because they cannot be tested; it is certainly not because the answers do not matter.

Knowledge of the existence within towns of localities where there is a high degree of poverty in its various forms does not depend on the analysis of statistics; it is a matter of observation. Perhaps the credit for transforming that observation into a matter of policy should go to the Plowden Council on primary schooling,[9] which suggested special treatment ('positive discrimination') for the schools in such localities. But although the Council's own recommendation was based on observation, it suggested that available statistics on the local incidence of some socio-economic problems should be analysed in order to pinpoint exactly which localities should qualify as Educational Priority Areas. The specific indicators suggested were:

Occupation
Size of families
Supplements in cash or kind from the state
Overcrowding and sharing houses
Poor attendance and truancy
Proportions of retarded, disturbed or handicapped pupils
Incomplete families
Children unable to speak English

Since then a number of authorities have made statistical analyses on an area-by-area basis, either for the specific purpose of locating E.P.A.s,[10] or for more general analytic or planning purposes,[11] or with the distribution of personal social services in mind,[12] and there are numerous examples of a specific area that has been seen to be deprived being compared with the rest of the city to demonstrate the many ways in which it is worse than average.

All these statistical exercises succeed in demonstrating the existence of worse-off localities within a local authority area; and in general they confirm that such localities are often to be found in the older, more central, parts of a city. But, while they are of great short-term value for the authority's task of planning, allocating resources, identifying problems and drawing attention to policy requirements, they do not, and cannot, answer some of the longer-term sociological questions that are asked of them. The problem seems to arise from the attempt to short-cut the analysis by looking directly at summary statistics for each *area*, without first forming any hypothesis about *people*. Multivariate analysis of individuals raises some difficult conceptual problems: when it attacks predefined groups of individuals, these problems are compounded. We seem to be trying to measure something without knowing what it is we are trying to measure. If, on the other hand, the analysis could be based initially on individual people or households, it would then be a rather simpler matter to compare the spatial distribution of the various types that might be identified.

Not that these 'ecological' analyses are devoid of interest. In particular, measurements of the apparent association, or lack of it, between the incidence of various problems can show whether it is reasonable, *prima facie*, to look for one type of problem area or different types. For instance, in Monmouthshire a distinction was made between areas of *economic* stress and of *social* stress.[13]

Indicators of economic stress	Indicators of social stress
School clothing allowance	Psychiatric patients
All unemployed	Juvenile crime – malicious damage
Females unemployed	Adult crime – assault
Overcrowding	Juvenile cautions
Unemployed aged 15-24	Children E.S.N. and handicapped
Males unemployed	Abortions
Optical charges exemptions	School psychological service referrals
Supplementary Benefit	Divorce
(families in need)	Adult crime – other
Dental charges exemptions	Adult crime – major motoring offences

Prescription charges exemptions   Child guidance referrals
Free school meals
Supplementary Benefit
  (pensioners)

Confusingly to those living in areas where neither of these general problems is common, the same general area – the 'valleys' of east Monmouthshire – is above average in the incidence of both types of stress. But the analysis demonstrates that the localities where one problem is most acute are not the localities that suffer most acutely from the other. One implication is that there are two independent problems, which presumably invite different policies.

Although the example is derived from a county, not a city, the distinction between areas of economic stress and social stress mirrors a similar distinction between urban problem areas made by sociologists long before the current debate on urban multiple deprivation, but which seems to have had remarkably little effect on it.[14] The theory is expressed in terms of housing, though it could also be related to employment or other key motivators. On the one hand, it identifies *residual* areas: parts of the city where the working class has been in occupation for generations, probably in houses originally designed for them. The area is historically stable, and a societal network (often based on kinship ties) has grown up. The area is, however, on the way down, principally as a result of the physical decay of the buildings. The residents want to get out. On the other hand, the theory identifies *transitional* areas. These are places newly occupied by people who have not yet established a place in the city's society, often migrants from this country or abroad, or individuals who are in the process of a sharp change in social role. Such areas usually grow up where the middle classes are giving up their large and ageing houses, which become suitable for flats and bedsitters at minimum conversion costs and high rents. Only a loose society exists. The residents, who have only just arrived, are not particularly keen to get out.

It is, of course, not possible rigidly to divide every part of every city into one or the other of these categories. In London it is possible to identify mainly residual areas (in the East End) and mainly transitional areas (Notting Hill). There are also places that were transitional in the last generation and have now become residual (parts of Islington?), and places where residuality has opened up scope for transition (Brixton?). Perhaps if both processes are at work at the same time, with transitional people occupying the houses deserted by the residual people fortunate enough to escape, a very special problem arises. Nevertheless, at the individual level it is desirable to distinguish between those who are on their way down, and perhaps out, and those who are on their way in, and perhaps up. But, by covering both with the term 'deprivation', there is the risk of confusing two problems, both analytically and politically. The fact that neither problem appears to affect the stable middle class or the stable working class does not mean that both are the same problem. But the combination of total lack of hygiene facilities (mainly a residual problem) with non-English-speaking migrants (transitional) in the designation of E.P.A.s suggests analytical confusion; and the choice of both types of area for Community Development Projects suggests confusion in policy – unless, of course, the theoretical distinction is rejected.

If it is not rejected, it is worth pursuing a little further, for it helps to explain the distinction between material stress and social stress mentioned earlier. Residual areas inherit a stable working-class society, which enables most of the residents to cope socially and psychologically with the deterioration in their housing and/or employment opportunities, the material matters that are their main problem. In transitional areas, on the other hand, the housing is not always totally inadequate – at least the fact that the residents have just moved in suggests some sort of acceptance of it, if only for the lack of any alternative. Moreover, their employment opportunities are not necessarily restricted – most may have jobs, and many may have good jobs. The problem is that there is no developed society to uphold the individual in trouble. Indeed, many of the newly-arrived residents will have come precisely because they already have a social or psychological problem that has caused them either to seek asylum from the rigid morality of more stable societies, or to seek shelter as a last resort after rejection by society. The tendency for unmarried mothers to lose themselves in the anonymity of city centres illustrates this. Thus, either because the residents are self-selected social misfits or because there is no help from local society, the transitional area shows more social than material problems. It can be argued from these distinctions that the problems of residual areas need to be cured altogether, so that residual areas cease to exist, but that transitional areas fill a genuine social need; far from being eliminated, they should be helped to fill the need more effectively. Such areas perform a role exactly analogous to the role played so vitally, if inadequately, by furnished accommodation. Of course, it is precisely in these areas that the furnished accommodation is to be found.

Both these types of area have been defined principally in terms of the relation between people and housing. Housing is probably the key item in dividing cities into residential areas of varying character. Since housing has tended in the past to be built in areas at a specific point in time, for a specific class,* the houses in an area will tend to grow old and obsolete** at about the same period, encouraging a similar compartmentalisation in society. But it is also important to consider the position of employment in respect of such areas.

It will already be clear that the problems of deprived areas are largely problems of *change*, whether the change is principally concerned with decline and absolute obsolescence (residual) or with immigration or a general state of flux (transitional). In the field of employment we can see similar processes at work. On the one hand, there are areas of old-established industry that is in the process of outwearing its economic profitability, its old premises or its old technology. Any of these factors will mean a decline in the employment prospects for those who previously depended on it, leading to migration away from the area for some, or unemployment, low wages and insecurity for the remainder. Uncompensated decline in a previously stable industry can be seen in the same light as housing decay.

On the other hand, areas of new or increasing prosperity, with increasing need for workers, will tend to create a situation likely to encourage in-migration, pressure on housing space, and the formation of transitional areas.

It would be wrong, however, to conclude that residual areas are confined to towns of declining prosperity, or transitional areas to growth towns. In every large town, as in the country as a whole, there will be some industries in decline and others growing. If both industries depend on similar types of labour, the transition could be reasonably smooth, as workers transfer from one to the other. But if the growth industry requires a different type of labour, the conditions for both residual and transitional problems have been created. This is

---

*This ignores the question of why new houses should have been compartmented in this way, but that is a historical question in this context.
**Either totally obsolete (residual) or obsolete for its original class or purpose (transitional).

likely, as the economic trend is away from manual labour requiring strength towards more skilful non-manual occupations. Indeed, technological change can lead to the conflicting problems of decline and growth in the demands for various kinds of labour occurring within the same industry, and within the same firm. Thus both types of social problem can co-exist within the same town, or even within the same locality. On the other hand, where a whole town is dependent on industries in decline and no compensatory growth occurs, then it is likely that a large proportion of that town, or even the town as a whole, could be classified as 'residual'. A number of northern industrial towns can be said to be in this predicament.

Employment or unemployment can be seen to have an important role to play in the formation of areas of acute urban deprivation. It is unlikely, however, to be able to play the decisive role in the tight geographical concentration of deprived people within cities. People rarely do their work in their homes, and the distances that most are prepared to travel to work would take them beyond the boundaries of the small zones of acute deprivation that have been identified within cities. If unemployment, or low-status employment (measured on the basis of where people live, instead of where they work), are more heavily concentrated in one locality than another, it is not possible to find an explanation simply in terms of the general industrial health of the locality, for industry has a wider catchment area. This can be illustrated in Paisley, a town probably small enough (24,000 economically active males) to function as a single employment area, where distance from employment opportunities is not an important factor in influencing the ability of individuals to find work. Yet the unemployment rate in the Ferguslie Park district is 22 per cent, compared with an average of 8 per cent in the town as a whole.[15] Once such a situation has developed, the adverse reputation of the area may make it even more difficult for its residents to find work.

Similarly, employment prospects in the Small Heath area of inner Birmingham cannot be ascribed simply to a lack of jobs, when thousands of people have excellent jobs in central Birmingham – within walking distance of Small Heath.[16] Thus the tendency of deprived people to congregate in small areas is primarily a *residential* function. We can then examine the neighbouring employment opportunities for those sorts of people to explain the extent of their *economic* deprivation. That means looking at the characteristics of the people, as well as those of the jobs available, to seek an explanation for the evident mismatch between local supply and demand for particular types of job that has occurred. For some reason the jobs and the people are not suited to each other. An explanation could be offered partly in terms of unpleasant social functions – idleness or incompetence in the people, racial or social discrimination by the employers – but operational functions are probably more important – the jobs available locally are not the sort of jobs the people have been trained to do.

In many cases this operational mismatch can in turn be explained by local or national change in the structure of employment, as the demand for labour changes qualitatively faster than the supply. But that does not imply that the phenomenon is temporary, and will go away as the change works its way through; for the changes themselves are permanently repetitive. But this conclusion should not in turn indicate that the social problems of change are unavoidable or incapable of alleviation. It should be possible to make marginal effects by, for instance, management of transport policy to make job opportunities available over a wider area. Secondly, it may be possible to damp the pace of local change, either by bolstering up declining local industries while their workers age themselves out of the workforce, or by encouraging employers of similar types of labour to replace them. Thirdly, and most positively, it should be possible to accept the change in industry but work to prevent ill-effects on workers, through active labour market policies. This means taking positive action to encourage mobility between houses and between jobs, in particular by training workers from declining industries in the skills required in the growth sectors. This is one of the key conclusions from PEP's continuing programme of research on labour market policy.[17] Such policy not only encourages the economic benefits to be derived from industrial change, and not only prevents workers and their families from suffering in consequence, but it enables the people to obtain some of the economic benefits for themselves.

In 1969 the Home Office began to set up a series of Community Development Projects in twelve acutely depressed localities, in order to see whether detailed consideration of local problems, or intense local activity, could find a solution to their deprivation. Although the members of these teams continue to work actively and sympathetically in their districts, the principal conclusion of their first review of the project as a whole seems to suggest that such work is incapable of having the desired effect.[18] It is pointed out that the problems of these districts are not the fault of the residents, but are the outcome of economic changes beyond the control either of the residents or of any purely local agency.* Neither of those conclusions is much questioned. The suggestion that the social sins of the people were responsible for a Welsh coal seam running out has a biblical ring to it; it surely was not seriously put forward. But the following conclusion, that only a direct reversal of the economic causes can solve the problem, is less certainly acceptable. An attack on the first original cause of a phenomenon is not the only way of tackling it. If we were concerned that people got wet when it rained, we would not attempt to stop the rain but would take steps to provide shelter. If we ask why the original cause (economic change) led to a social problem, we may find that the people affected were prevented from making an acceptable adjustment to the change. In this case a solution based on an examination of local circumstances might call for provision of bus services to centres of employment, provision of assistance to those who might benefit from moving home, the encouragement of industries using the right kind of labour, or the provision of retraining with generous allowances. In some of the C.D.P. areas (e.g. Glyncorrwg and Cleator Moor), which are small towns, almost villages, that have lost their industrial *raison d'être* and have an absolute lack of accessible employment, more radical solutions might be necessary. In others, prosperity is sufficiently close at hand for local adjustments to be beneficial. (This is not to suggest that industrial location policy is irrelevant to such problems – far from it – but to point out that it is not the only possible activity, nor necessarily the vital one.) The argument does not apply simply to employment.

Perhaps the key question that remains unanswered concerns the functional relation between geographical and personal characteristics. Much study has been devoted to the existence of various social problems and their distribution among individuals. More recently there has been discussion of the distribution of a range of social problems between areas. What is lacking is a constructive synthesis between these two streams of thought that would determine how far geographical problems have influenced individuals in the past, and how far geographical policies can be made to influence them in future.

---

*This conclusion is considered so fundamental that it is reiterated at least eight separate times in the C.D.P.'s second joint publication![19]

In so far as the question has been discussed at all, it has been dominated by several clichés, which, perhaps like all clichés, have exaggerated tendencies into laws.

For a few years now, perhaps ever since the Plowden Council's report in 1966, there has been a tendency for discussion of the geographical aspects of poverty to assume that deprived people and deprived areas were virtually the same problem. A superficial knowledge of the discussion might have given the impression that all deprived people lived in deprived areas; conversely, that deprived areas were inhabited exclusively by deprived people; and, thirdly, that a solution to the geographical problem would eliminate the problem experienced by individuals. It has already been pointed out (Chapter 4) that the Plowden hypothesis of concentration was not backed by factual analysis, and that it has recently been shown that most of inner London's deprived children do not live in deprived areas, and that most of the children in such areas are not deprived.[20] A fairly strong swing in the pendulum is now in progress. The data on the location of deprived children have been used to argue that the Educational Priority Area policy is badly aimed. Analysis of census data for small areas (enumeration districts) has shown that although there is a tendency for sufferers of any particular kind of deprivation to be found together in the same place, and a tendency for one kind of deprivation to be found in the same places as other kinds of deprivation, by the time the two tendencies have been added together the vast majority of deprived households are not to be found in the multiply-deprived small areas.[21] Again, analysis of variations in income for households and for small areas (wards) in Greater London shows that the variation among households within each ward is almost as great as variation across the whole of the capital.[22] The G.L.C. would have to cover 38 per cent of all wards, covering 1,000,000 households, in order to cover half (300,000) of the households with gross incomes below £1,000 (1971-72). Nor, according to that analysis, does inner London contain all that high a proportion of such households.

On the whole, therefore, it seems that geographical concentration, and the 'inner city' thesis, are not as important to an analysis of deprivation as it was thought. On the other hand, it is important not to let this swing of the pendulum go so far as to discount geographical considerations altogether. There is obviously *something* about the inner city. Nearly three-quarters of all commonwealth immigrants, a group of very high deprivation risk, live in only 10 per cent of the country's enumeration districts.[23] In all the large conurbations these areas of high immigrant concentration are more likely to be found in the older, inner parts of the city.[24] Areas that score high on 'multiple deprivation' are also more likely to be found in the inner city. Similarly, the analysis of London's income patterns (mentioned above), which showed that inner London did not have all that many poor *people*, nevertheless found a sufficient spatial split for an inner ring of London to account for over 94 per cent of the capital's relatively poor *wards* against only 40 per cent of its population.[25]

Thus, although geography is by no means the whole of the problem, it does seem that in certain parts of many of our largest towns and cities there are certain special processes at work: processes which, although apparently slight if studied one at a time, are nevertheless sufficiently powerful in combination to reach take-off point, and to make multiple deprivation a special problem. On the present evidence, therefore, a special multi-policy attack on housing, employment, education and so on does seem to be required for such areas, provided the wider problem is faced as well. Perhaps it would be fair to say that deprivation is partly a matter of *who you are*, and partly a matter of *where you live*.

In this context it may be useful to note that the concentration of poverty is not the only inequality in inequality. In many areas, especially in central London and some of its more exclusive suburbs, may be found pockets of acute concentration of rich people. A count of Rolls-Royces in Belgravia will easily demonstrate that. Yet it has not been suggested that residence in these areas makes people rich; nor has it been suggested that policy in such areas could do much to damage their excessive richness!

If it is important to discover the nature and extent of the role of spatial factors in deprivation, then it will be necessary first to define and analyse deprivation as it affects individual people, and then to look at the way the problem is spread among different localities. There is one school of thought whose advocates are reluctant to bring the analysis of deprivation down to the level of the individual, lest it should be inferred that it is the individual who is personally responsible for his plight; a purely geographical analysis is therefore adopted in order to suggest external geographical causes that do not imply personal criticism. Because people can and do move across geographical boundaries, however, social geography must start with people. Nor does an explanation of why a particular man or family is deprived necessarily imply that he or they are responsible; since inevitably certain individuals are responsible for their plight, it is useless to exclude that possibility in advance, but there are many sources of inequality, some of which have been considered in this report, which operate at the individual level without being self-inflicted. In fact the main objection to the ecological approach runs contrary to the ideals of those same sympathetic analysts who adopt it. To consider deprivation primarily as a geographical phenomenon is to suggest that geography is the primary cause of the problem, and that geographical policies might largely eliminate it. A personal analysis would show that deprivation is a problem whose seriousness runs much, much deeper than that.

NOTES

1 See B. Coates and E. Rawstron, *Regional Variations In Britain*, Batsford, 1971.
2 C. Moser and W. Scott (*British Towns*, Oliver and Boyd, 1961) provide a detailed statistical analysis of variations between towns, and a typology, although the data are now twenty-five years old.
3 e.g. M. Meacher. 'Scrooge Areas', *New Society*. 2 Dec. 1971.
4 Phyllis Willmott, 'Health and Welfare', in M. Young (ed.), *Poverty Report 1974*, Maurice Temple Smith, 1974.
5 B. Davies, *Social Needs and Resources in Local Authority Services*, Michael Joseph, 1968; and J. Packman, *Child Care: Needs and Numbers*. N.I.S.W., 1968.
6 T. Blackstone (*A Fair Start*, Penguin, 1972) gives an account of how different local authorities have tackled, or failed to tackle, one service – in this case, nursery schooling.
7 Coates and Rawstron, *op. cit*; Phyllis Willmott *op. cit.*
8 Dept. of Health and Social Security, *Health and Personal Social Services Statistics for England 1974*, H.M.S.O., 1974.
9. Central Advisory Council for Education (England), *Children and Their Primary Schools*, (the Plowden Report), H.M.S.O., 1967.
10 For instance, the I.L.E.A. See A. Little and C. Mabey, 'An Index for the Designation of Educational Priority Areas', in A. Shonfield and S. Shaw (eds), *Social Indicators and Social Policy*, Heinemann, 1972.

11 See e.g. M. Harris, 'Some Aspects of Social Polarisation', in D. Donnison and D. Eversley (eds), *London: Urban Patterns, Problems and Policies*, Heinemann, 1973.

12 For instance, in Liverpool: see M. Flynn *et al*, 'Social Malaise Research: a study in Liverpool', in *Social Trends*, No. 3, H.M.S.O. 1972. Also in Southwark: see S. Hatch and R. Sherrott, 'Positive Discrimination and the Distribution of Deprivation', *Policy and Politics*, vol. 1, No. 3, March 1973.

13 J. Kegie and D. G. Thomas, 'Social Malaise Study: an interim report on the distribution of social problems', *Clearing House for Local Authority Social Services Research*, No. 8, July 1974.

14 See C. Vereker *et al*, *Urban Redevelopment and Social Change*, Liverpool University Press, 1961.

15 Paisley Community Development Project, *Initial Report*, mimeo.

16 See various reports on the Birmingham Inner Area Study (Llewellyn-Davis, Weeks, Forestier-Walker, and Bor) published by the Dept. of the Environment.

17 See especially S. Mukherjee, *Making Labour Markets Work*, PEP Broadsheet No. 532, 1972.

18 The National Community Development Project, *Inter-Project Report*, C.D.P. Information and Intelligence Unit, Centre for Environmental Studies, 1974.

19 The National Community Development Project, *Forward Plan, 1975-76*, C.D.P. Information and Intelligence Unit, 1975

20 See J.H. Barnes and H. Lucas, 'Positive Discrimination in Education: Individuals, Groups and Institutions', in J. H. Barnes (ed.), *Educational Priority Vol. 3*, H.M.S.O., 1975.

21 S. Holterman, *Census Indicators of Urban Deprivation, Working Note No. 6, Great Britain*, Dept. of the Environment, 1975.

22 R. Berthoud, 'Where are London's poor?', forthcoming.

23 S. Holterman, *op. cit.*

24 S. Holterman, *Census Indicators of Urban Deprivation, Working Note No. 10, The Conurbations of Great Britain*, Dept. of the Environment, 1975.

25 R. Berthoud, *op. cit.*

7   What is Deprivation?

In order to reach some general conclusions about the relation between deprivation and inequality, it will be useful to consider some of the main points arising from our review of the particular aspects of the problem.

Review

Inequality
Although increasing prosperity provides benefits for all of us, it does not appear to have had much effect on the degree of inequality. There are still many people who have so much less than the rest of the population that they must be considered to remain in poverty. Although hardly anyone believes that it is desirable, still less possible, to aim to achieve total equality, it is widely believed that the range of inequality is too great. Deprivations might therefore be considered to be those aspects of inequality that are avoidable: if we can do without them, they are unnecessary, and consequently unfair. It is possible to consider two strategies for the attack on unnecessary inequality.

1 One strategy would be to tackle the whole structure of inequality from top to bottom. The reduction of inequalities of opportunity in the job market should reduce inequalities in earnings, at the same time as increasing the output of the system as a whole.
2 The second strategy would be to strike directly at the lowest end of inequality, wherever this is possible without interfering with the market, in which general inequality provides the driving force through incentives. Thus, although it is difficult to imagine a society in which a roadsweeper earns as much as a brain surgeon, there is no reason why they should not both enjoy the same conditions of service, and both look forward to an old age in which their style of life is not restricted by too sharp a fall in purchasing power.

These strategies are not mutually exclusive; either or both could be employed wherever possible in policies to eliminate deprivation.

Social Security

Provision of social security is obviously one of the main policies within the second strategy. Although around 1950 our social security may have been one of the best in the world, it is now due for another fundamental rethink, as comprehensive as that undertaken by Lord Beveridge. It has become so fragmented, with so many different benefits, with different rules, applying to different people, that it is no longer clear exactly what it is trying to achieve. Whatever the aim, it is clearly failing to achieve it, since a great many of the provisions are not being used by the people who are entitled to them. But reform is needed not only to clarify existing aims, not only to ensure that those aims are efficiently achieved, but also to review the aims themselves. Our social security is intended to provide only a rock bottom minimum; the extra income required for a decent level of living is left to 'individual initiative'. For most people individual initiative does not, and perhaps cannot, provide that extra income. And since the great majority of people provided with the rock bottom minimum are not in the labour market, it is unnecessary (and therefore unfair) to justify such low levels of provision in terms of the work incentive. Nor does the continuing distinction between insurance and welfare any longer make sense. There are signs of the beginnings of progress in these directions, but there is a long way to go.

Housing

In housing policy the strategy for eliminating deprivation needs to be thought out very carefully. There has been undoubted progress in the quantity and the quality of the housing stock over the years. It will, of course, be necessary to continue with this improvement, as housing standards rise with increasing prosperity; nevertheless, on an aggregate view, the housing situation is better than it used to be. Yet, perversely, something seems to have gone wrong. The housing needs of the elderly are not being met. The intense concentration of housing problems among families of Asian and West Indian origin perhaps suggests that they have been landed with a new housing problem, as well as taking over the old one; and the continuing, increasing problem of homelessness (in which the racial minorities are again over-represented) indicates the failure of owner-occupation and council housing to solve housing problems in a flexible way. In the end the long-term solution to housing problems may lie not in housing policy itself but in geographical planning policy. Housing problems will continue until the distribution of houses, jobs and people has been brought into balance.

Children

The problems of children and of educational policy, and their roles in perpetuating social and economic inequality, are much less clearly identifiable. It is by now sufficiently well established that reduced material circumstances play a part in reduced educational achievement; it is time to make sure that unfair differences in the circumstances of different families are dealt with. Yet, as was noted in Chapter 1, that cannot be done until a combination of research and public debate has suggested what differences are fair or unfair, and what effect a resolution of the differences would have on people's behaviour. If Belgium can offer family allowances three to four times as high as ours,[1] without encouraging excessive child-bearing or discouraging work, there does not seem to be any reason why Britain could not do the same.

Education itself is a much more difficult issue. Educational success is not vital to success in employment (41 per cent of male 'employers and managers' have no formal educational qualification, and 43 per cent of those with such qualifications are manual workers[2]); but it clearly helps. Similarly, educational failure is not an inevitable consequence of a low-status background, but there is a close connection. And if it is true, as recent analyses have indicated, that the characteristics of a school have little influence on the quality of its output, it becomes doubtful whether the school is doing any more than sorting the sheep from the goats. The great reform of comprehensive secondary education may do little more than paper over the cracks of educational inequality.

Our educational system often seems to be mainly interested in identifying those who can 'get ahead', devoting a larger and larger proportion of the resources to them at each successive stage. The inevitable converse is that the rest are left behind. Although it is not intended that such a system should favour the middle classes, that is what happens. Ironically, qualifications by examination, which were invented to eradicate unfair privilege of the upper class with respect to the middle class, are now favouring the middle class with respect to the lower. But even if this class bias is left out of the argument, an education system designed to separate out the clever from the dull, in order to promote the cleverness of the former, provides the sub-structure for inequality in employment.

For just over a century we have tried, and failed, to reduce the gap in educational opportunity. If we cannot equalise opportunity in education, perhaps we should try, instead, to provide actual equality in education, in an attempt to equalise opportunity in the labour market. This is a radical solution, but not to be dismissed out of hand if education is really intended as a means to greater equality.

Employment

The analysis of employment highlights the old story of inequalities between manual workers and non-manual workers, and between unskilled manual workers at one extreme and managerial and professional workers at the other. It is not suggested that there should be identical pay for widely different jobs, but the range of inequality and the variety of its facets does seem to be excessive. Some of the inequality could be removed without undermining the driving power of the incentive differential; and if that could be done successfully, the re-movable aspects could be considered unnecessary and therefore unfair.

Earlier in this summary it was suggested that there were two possible strategies for the attack on excessive inequality: tackling the main structure, or striking especially at the lower end. In the case of employment both strategies are appropriate. If part of the explanation for the limited access to high-status jobs lies in artificial restrictions imposed, not necessarily deliberately, by the education system or by recruitment procedures, then a removal of those restrictions ought to free the labour market to find a more equitable equilibrium. As the competition for high-status jobs increased, and as the supply of men willing to perform low-status jobs dried up, the earnings differential ought to diminish.

Within each of the two broad occupational groups there remain inequalities that could be reduced. Mobility between clerical and managerial/professional occupations is also limited, and male clerical workers' earnings may be undermined by the huge pool of female labour, available at discriminatorily low wages. Within the manual group there are signs that mobility between occupations and between industries is so difficult that a worker may become trapped in a job of declining economic value. By the time he reaches his forties his wages begin to decline relative to those of younger men. The reluctance of employers to recruit and train middle-aged men leaves him with little room to manoeuvre. Active labour market policies to promote free movement within and between the occupational groups should do much to alter the structure of inequality.

But the direct-strike strategy will also be essential. At first sight a disadvantage faced by most manual workers, who constitute a majority of the workforce, scarcely merits a label so extreme as 'deprivation'. But it is in their greater risk of sudden and extreme misfortune – through redundancies, the sack, unemployment and, eventually, in old age – that manual workers are most at a disadvantage with respect to managerial and professional workers. If conditions of service were equalised by law, and, above all, if everyone could look forward to retirement without fear of poverty, many of the most serious social problems discussed in this book would be diminished. There is no concrete evidence that such action would have unfortunate side-effects.

The Geography of Poverty

In spite of the enormous interest in the spatial distribution of deprivation over the past ten years, we are not much nearer a real understanding of the phenomenon; nor has a policy been developed to deal with it. It is, however, becoming clear that pockets of multiple deprivation in the inner areas of older cities, or elsewhere, do not cover anywhere near the whole of the more general problem of unnecessary inequality in society. Nevertheless, the evidence suggests that there is a special process at work, as a result of which a series of individually minor forces combine to constitute a serious problem. In so far as it is possible to determine the nature of those forces, it is reasonable to believe that a multi-policy attack on this inequality in inequality would result, not in a redistribution of the same problems to other parts of the country, but in a net reduction in the general level of deprivation. The attack must be not only in these localities themselves, but also in the wider field of planning a more stable equilibrium in the location of people, homes, jobs and public services.

Health

One major form of deprivation has not been assigned a separate chapter in this report. Health problems have been omitted not because they are unimportant, but because it is impossible for a social researcher with no medical training to accord them even the brief treatment given to other more purely social kinds of disadvantage. But since there are over three million handicapped and impaired adults in Great Britain,[3] and a further three million who report a long-standing illness which limits their activities;[4] since acute illnesses and premature deaths continue to impose suffering on a large number of people, there are certain points about health problems which do require attention in this review of deprivation, even if physiological questions are left aside.

Ill-health – particularly long-term ill-health or disablement – causes problems which are too obvious to require detailed discussion here.[5] There are the difficulties inherent in the disease or handicap itself; there are the social problems inflicted both on the patient and his family and friends; and there are financial problems resulting both from partial or total loss of earning power, and from increased outlay. In these senses, people suffering from ill-health are undoubtedly 'deprived', and on these grounds alone we could call for continued progress in medical services, both preventative and curative, and improved social services to palliate the effects of long-term illness. In the context of this study, however, it is important to know whether those deprived of good health should be considered as part of the main-stream of the deprived class, or whether they should be tacked on as the result of physiological accident.

That question needs to be introduced by looking first at current trends in the overall picture. It may well be that the nation's health – on the whole – is improving year by year, as with average wages, the real value of social security benefits, housing conditions, and educational attainments. This is certainly true if we look at mortality statistics – average life expectancy continues to rise, if not so fast as in the first half of the century, and, conversely, death rates for each age group fall, including infants.[6] In the case of the incidence of long-term sickness we cannot be so sure. Good general statistics have only recently been collected; if we had a series we would have difficulty in deciding whether or not to allow for the increasing number of elderly people, or for increased chronic morbidity figures caused directly by greater success in saving life.

It was the dreadful prevalence of disease in urban slums which first awoke the social conscience of the middle classes in the 1830s and 1840s. Even at the beginning of this century it was the need to examine social variations in mortality and morbidity that prompted the invention of the Social Class classification of occupations – the forerunner of the classification used so much in this report. Yet today, with improved medical techniques, adequate diets, and a free health service, surely illness has now become a physiological accident, with social consequences, of course, but not social origins.

Not so: where statistics are available over a long period of years, there is no evidence that the general improvement in health has been accompanied by a reduction in variations between social classes: although the figures are not exactly comparable, it appears that variation got worse and worse between the early 1930s and the early 1960s, and is not really getting better again.

Table 37 Male standardised mortality rates*, by social class[7]

	1921-23 (age 20-64)	1930-32 (age 20-64)	1949-53 (age 20-64)	1959-63 (age 15-64)	1970-72 (age 15-64)
Professional	82	90	86	76	77
Managerial Clerical/ Skilled manual	94	94	92	81	81
	95	97	101	100	104
Semi-skilled manual	101	102	104	103	113
Unskilled manual	125	111	118	143	137

*S.M.R. gives the extent to which each class's mortality rate was greater (over 100) or less (below 100) than the average, after taking account of the age structure of each class.

One could almost say that 23 per cent of all deaths to men in the prime of life could be attributed to differences in social class.

There are plenty of other figures which show how much more prone to illness are members of the less prosperous groups:

Table 38 Various health problems, by social class[8]

	Man./ Prof.	Clerical	Skilled Manual	Semi- Skilled	Unskilled Manual
Mortality, males aged 15-64*	80	104		113	137
Stillbirths and perinatal deaths (Scotland)	2.5%	3.3%		3.7%	4.8%
Limiting long-standing illness* (England & Wales)	75	86	104	120	137
Acute sickness* (England & Wales)	89	95	101	111	135

*Age standardised rates, compared with average.

While in some cases, ill health may lead someone to take up a lower grade job than he would take if he was healthy, this cannot explain away most of these differences. It must be the other way round: evidently there is something about those with high status jobs that makes them, or their families, more healthy than those in low status jobs.

Without attempting to guess what this 'something' is, we can use these figures to go straight back to the central theme of this report. Members of privileged groups are not free from health problems; nor need members of disadvantaged groups look forward to inevitable sickness, disability and early death. It will usually be an 'accident' that determines whether any individual member of any group succumbs to sickness, but some groups get far more than their share of these problems. Research in the health field is desperately needed to find out how this happens; but at the same time, health has turned out to be yet another facet of more general inequalities in society.

Discussion

If it was necessary to summarise 'deprivation' in a few words, one would at first be hard put to it to be more precise than describing it as an umbrella to cover all the various misfortunes people can suffer in society. Indeed, a historical perspective might lead us to conclude that deprivation is a phenomenon that has arisen in the field of political thought; a view of the way society works, in relation to how it ought to work, as much as a phenomenon existing in society itself. Two hundred years of industrial prosperity, and a hundred and fifty years of public concern for the welfare of 'the masses', have led to a new emphasis on the need to ensure the welfare of minorities. There is a popular cry currently that 'the poor are getting poorer'. Although there is some evidence that this may be happening in an objective sense, the cry has most meaning in the sense that the poverty of the poor is becoming more unacceptable to society as a whole. While there are differences of opinion as to what is and is not acceptable, there is a growing determination that positive, perhaps very radical, action is needed to ensure that no one should remain unacceptably worse-off than the rest of us.

If that is to be achieved, however, it is necessary to examine the concept in greater depth, in order to understand how the situation continues, and to try to assess the possible effects on all groups in society of any policies that might be proposed.

Perhaps a helpful way of approaching 'deprivation' as a single concept would be to ask in what sense we could describe 'the deprived' as a single group in society. Starting from a list of social misfortunes, we can see a whole range of problems not necessarily suffered in combination by the same people. We can identify those with poor jobs, or those who are repeatedly without jobs; those who depend on social security; those in poor housing; those whose children receive a poor education; those who suffer poor health; and so on. Thus there are many different problems. Similarly, taking any one problem, we can list different types of people who suffer – old-age pensioners, unsupported mothers, large families, and so on. All this may suggest an unconnected maze of traps into which people or families may fall for a variety of reasons. But it is possible to describe some very broad groups of people for whom deprivations of every sort are not so much a possibility as a probability; and from this evident concentration to derive hypotheses about the origins of the problems, the links between them, and the extent of *multiple* deprivation.

The class of people who have far, far more than their share of social problems is the elderly. People aged 65 or over constitute 13 per cent of the total population but suffer 37 per cent of the chronic illness,[9a] 60 per cent of physical handicaps and 75 per cent of the very severe handicaps.[9b] 52 per cent of elderly families, against 18 per cent of all families, are living at, or no more than 10 per cent above, Supplementary Benefit level.[9c] Small elderly households and single old people constitute 31 per cent of all households, but between them account for 52 per cent of the homes with no bath, and 49 per cent of the homes with an outside lavatory.[9d] There are over two million elderly people living all alone in private households,[9e] without either the emotional support of companionship or physical help in case of accident. There are nearly a quarter of a million elderly people living in hospital, and a similar number in other institutions.[9f] Only 30 per cent of old couples, and a mere 6 per cent of single old people, have a car to get about in.[9g] In all these cases, as in the last, single old people are even worse off than couples, concentrating the problem still more heavily on the older than average, who are mostly women. It takes no stretch of the imagination to conclude that there must be thousands and thousands of old women, living alone, with a physical handicap, in poverty, with inadequate sanitary facilities and no means of getting about; and hundreds of thousands of old people whose situation is not far short of this total catastrophe.

This situation is intolerable, and it will get worse numerically as a greater and greater proportion of the population survives into old age. Some of the problems may be unpreventable; some of them may not even be ameliorable; but others are open to action. It may be that in every society there must be some on the fringes who cannot enjoy a full share in its prosperity; but old people are on the fringe only because we leave them there. They are our own parents and grandparents; their plight is a foretaste of our own situation in ten, twenty or fifty years time; yet for some of them, their only Christmas present is a bag of sugar donated by the local Round Table. They are, or should be, mainstream members of society, but they are left defenceless by their age and by the exclusive principles of our social institutions. This is especially so for old women, who are rewarded for a lifetime of service to their husbands and families by being left helpless when their husbands depart – so helpless that many occupational pensions contain no provisions for widows. These are the people who are being talked about, when it is asserted that deprivations could easily be averted if only people were more prudent during their working lives.

The early boast of the welfare state was that it would care for people 'from the cradle to the grave'. In view of the facts just quoted, the second half of that catchphrase has a hollow ring. Other countries look after their elderly, at least in terms of pensions, much better than we have done, and even recent increases for British pensioners have not greatly closed the gap (Table 39).

Table 39 Pension rights for the average ex-wage earner and his wife, 1971, as a percentage of average net earnings in 1970[10]

Netherlands	64.3
Germany	60.0
Belgium	56.8
France	51.5
Britain	35.1
Italy	33.3

Denmark's figure is probably very close to that of the Netherlands. Ireland's is probably lower than Britain's.

The relatively small population of old people accounts for perhaps half the incidence of each social problem, or deprivation, with which we are concerned (apart from those problems in work and education).

Because of this concentration of problems within a small group of people, it is probable that the incidence of *multiple* deprivation – of households suffering two, three or four problems all at once – is even more dominated by old people; say, for illustration, that perhaps 75 per cent or 80 per cent of the multiply-deprived are old. Does this suggest that multiple deprivation, the subject of this study, is a problem of old age? Or, alternatively, should we set aside multiple deprivation among the elderly as a separate issue, before examining the (much lower) incidence of deprivation in the rest of the population? There may be some areas (e.g. pensions) in which policy could directly aid the elderly in a way that is not so easy for the rest of the population. But, although note should be taken of the situation of the elderly both in analysis and in the formulation of policy, it should not be considered as a separate problem. Deprivation, and multiple deprivation, are the consequence of helplessness in a society that puts a premium on individual strength. The elderly suffer more often than the young and middle-aged because more of them are helpless, but it is essentially the same problem. Secondly, although retirement may often form a watershed in an individual's prosperity, many of the problems of the old are foreshadowed in the middle-aged – housing, ill-health, the earnings of manual workers, and so on. Thirdly, among the elderly, as among every other age group, the risk of deprivation will be largely determined by one's lifetime status in society. The seeds of deprivation are sown early; the fruit is borne in old age, if not before. If the scope of our analysis is widened to cover the whole

Table 40　Percentage incidence of various social problems by social group[11]

	Man./ prof.	Other non-manual	Skilled manual	Semi-skilled	Un-skilled
Housing					
(a) Insufficient bedrooms	3	4	8	8	8
(b) Insufficient amenities	5	12	12	18	21
Education					
(c) Poor reading ability (aged 11)	7	15	22	31	38
Health					
(d) Limiting long-standing illness (middle-aged men)	11	19	20	24	33
Employment					
(e) Unemployed	2	3	4	5	12
(f) Less than £45 p.w. (1974)	7	25	13	27	45
(g) Over 48 hours p.w.	5		27		
Capital					
(h) No savings at all	7	12	22	38	

population, it becomes clear that the risk of any deprivation you care to mention is greatest among those of low social status (Table 40):

Although Table 40 has been put together from various sources, and even covers various populations (see note 11), it is clear that these social problems (and others besides) are most likely to affect those of lower occupational status. If you added up the figures in each column, you would find that members of the managerial/professional group share, on average, one of these problems between two; members of the unskilled group by contrast, average well over two problems each. On the other hand, the distribution of social misfortune does not suddenly tip against the lowest class; taking one problem with another, the progression is fairly smooth from group to group. If, however, we take a few liberties with the statistics to calculate the odds of any individual having at least one of these problems,[12] we can see that social distinctions at the top end of the hierarchy are of greatest importance—the greatest difference is between the sub-groups within the non-manual middle class (Fig. 6).

Looked at in this way, it may be more appropriate to see the absence of deprivation as a privilege of the upper middle class than to

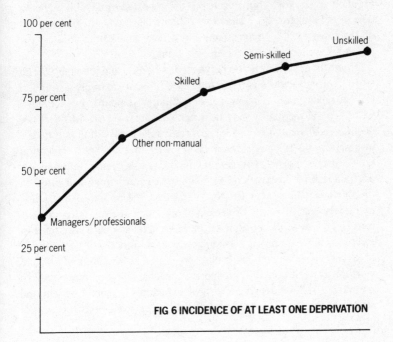

FIG 6 INCIDENCE OF AT LEAST ONE DEPRIVATION

view the presence of deprivation as a problem of the lower working class. The unskilled are not all that much more likely to be deprived than the manual working class as a whole.

On the other hand, the increasing concentration of each deprivation with lower social class provides good *prima facie* evidence for rapidly increasing *multiple* deprivation. Even if we assumed that within each class there was no tendency for problems to be associated with each other, the chances of finding an upper middle-class (professional/managerial) family with, for example, a chronically ill father earning less than £45 per week and a child who is a poor reader, are less than 1 in 2,000; in the unskilled group that chance of a threefold problem has risen to 56 in 1,000; i.e. the odds are that $5\frac{1}{2}$ per cent of the lowest class are in this situation.[13] The proportion will be higher if, as is probable, there are further correlations between problems within that class.

Deprivations, therefore, are problems that most commonly afflict people in the lower strata of society. But they are not exclusive to the very lowest stratum; the middle ranks are also affected, and even, occasionally, members of the highest rank. And multiple deprivation, probably even more concentrated in the lowest stratum, still seems to be a possibility for those higher up. Meanwhile, some members, even of the lowest class, may escape altogether, and suffer none of the problems we consider to be deprivations.

What, then, is the relation between deprivation and inequality? The word deprivation, as it is commonly used, appears to imply a situation that is unacceptably below some minimum standard, even though more general inequality may be accepted as at least inevitable, if not desirable. If inequality can be seen as a hill, deprivation is a ravine into which people should not be allowed to fall. The connection between the two is that general inequality is found to imply an unequal risk of deprivation. Although there are ravines that threaten the unwary walker near the top of the hill, the bottom of the hill is extremely hazardous, with ravines threatening at every step. So it is rare for those at the bottom of the hill to find a secure footing. For example, in Chapter 5 it was suggested that, although it was difficult to define the average day-to-day employment situation of manual workers as itself constituting deprivation, that situation represented a permanent risk of deprivation through sickness, unemployment and so on – a risk that is increasingly likely to be fulfilled as the worker grows older.

Thus it should be possible roughly to describe general types of people for whom the risk of all these misfortunes – single or multiple – is exceptionally high, and for whom the possibility of evasive or corrective action is limited. Classification by occupation is a convenient shorthand for social status, especially for the statistician, since most surveys include an analysis by occupation. But the best definition may not depend exclusively on this; considerations of geography, age, sex, marital status, ethnic origin and so on may come into it. Thus there is some evidence to suggest that the inhabitants of certain inner city areas are even more prone to deprivation than their occupational status would lead one to expect. Lone mother families are more at risk than lone father families.[14] Again, members of the racial minorities are at risk: their earnings are often lower than those of white men of comparable age and occupational level;[15] their children's reading scores are lower even than those of the unskilled workers' children;[16] and in spite of widespread owner-occupation, their housing conditions are considerably worse than those of unskilled workers.[17] Thus there is quite a range of people at risk, whose common link is their inability to preserve themselves from misfortune.

To change the analogy, we can see life as a game of pin-ball, where the scoring points represent deprivations (Fig. 7). When we play pin-ball, the exact score we achieve depends partly on chance and partly on the distribution of snares in the pin-ball machine. While some players have an easy machine, so that most of them score no deprivations at all, others have a different machine, in which many balls rattle from pillar to post, ringing up misfortune at every bounce.

This pin-ball analogy is surprisingly appropriate, for it holds up when we try to relate this theory of multiple risk to the other main theory of multiple deprivation – the theory of mutual causation, or the one-thing-leads-to-another theory. According to this explanation, if you start with, say, poor education, that leads to low income, which in turn leads to poor housing, which gives rise to ill-health, consequent unemployment, and thus Supplementary Benefit (a sequence that can be followed through the pin-ball machine in Fig. 7). This is what the Plowden Council described as the 'seamless web of circumstance'. The theory of risk is designed to complement, rather than supplant, the theory of mutual causation. It does have one advantage that purely causative theories lack. If we say that one problem causes another, it is difficult to accommodate exceptions to

LOWER STATUS PINBALL   **UPPER STATUS PINBALL**

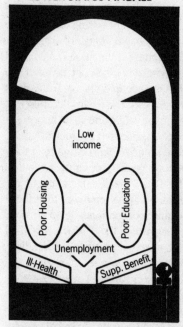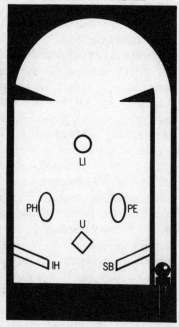

FIG 7 PINBALL ANALOGY

the rule without relying on another (hidden) pattern interfering with the dominant force. If we refer instead to risk, the exceptions are simply those cases where the risk is not fulfilled. The fact that not *all* people with bad jobs live in poor housing is thus no problem.

The two theories can be linked as follows: first, those of lower class have a high chance of suffering a first problem, which can then lead to others; and, secondly, even after the first problem is experienced, the causal link has a higher chance of connecting with the second problem. Thus, not only do manual workers have an above-average chance of suffering a physical injury at work, they also have an above-average chance of losing their job once injured. In the course of a recent, rather heated debate about the relation between social class and social misfortune, Sir Keith Joseph protested:

> It is because the children to whom I was referring are born to unmarried or single-parent teenage households, NOT, NOT, NOT because they are in socio-economic classes 4 and 5, that the children are at such risk of becoming tragedies in themselves and to society (original emphasis).[18]

The argument of this study is that, although illegitimate children may often be less happy than other members of their class of origin, children in the lower classes are not only rather more likely to be illegitimate but much more likely to suffer in consequence. It IS, IS, IS because they are in socio-economic classes 4 and 5 that the tragedies occur. Both the original risk and the consequent risk are greater.

More research is still needed into the direct causal links between one aspect of misfortune and another. One contribution to that end would be a comprehensive investigation of the extent to which any one particular misfortune afflicts the same people as any other, covering as wide a range of different types of problem as possible. It is necessary to know how far different problems coincide, not only through an overview of the whole of society but also on inspection in detail of different classes and sectors in society. In some cases no obvious direct connection can be assumed – for example, between physical incapacity in late middle-age and educational problems in childhood. In other cases a direct link may be more apparent – between low income and poor housing, for instance. On the other hand, it may be found that such obvious associations do not hold up when subjected to closer inspection: thus, although it is probably true that in London as a whole there is an association between low income and poor housing, it has been shown that in an area where both problems are common (Bethnal Green) there is no tendency for the worst-off for income to end up among the worst-off for housing.[19] Whatever the results of such detailed analysis, however, it seems likely that the main implications of the preceding paragraphs will provide a clue. The distributions of a number of apparently different, perhaps even unconnected, social misfortunes exhibit a remarkable similarity in unequally affecting people of unequal social status. The implication is that at least part of the explanation for deprivation, and for multiple deprivation, lies in that status itself.

Occupational status is a useful shorthand for social status, because it is closely connected with general social status, and because almost everyone can be ascribed an occupational status, either through his or her own job, or through the job of husband or father. According to the most recent census, the proportions of households whose chief economic supporter falls into each of the five main groups usually referred to in this book, are as follows.[20]

	per cent
Professional or managerial	15
Other non-manual	19
Skilled manual	32
Semi-skilled manual	15
Unskilled manual	6
(Armed forces, others	
not classified)	(13)

However, no shorthand can adequately represent the complexity of life as it actually happens. When the differences between classes are being discussed, it is easy to forget that by no means *all* the members of the 'top' class, however defined, exhibit the characteristics that are held to be typical of that class; similarly, not all members of the 'bottom' class are typical of it. Even within the group which, in previous chapters, has been given the top status there is variation between sections; the professionals tend to exhibit rather stronger evidence of middle-class culture, education and so on than the managers, but are not always more prosperous than them. Similarly, it can be argued that the unskilled group might really be divided between those of low skill level in a steady job, and those who cannot tie down a single steady job at all.[21]

When we try to assess the position of the other intermediate groups relative to the extremes, the problems of interpretation become even more difficult. Table 41 gives, for each of the five groups, a measure of their position, according to various types of information that provide a clear distinction between upper and lower classes.

According to the measures in Table 41, there is a wide gap between our 'top' and 'bottom' groups, and the intermediate groups come neatly in between. On the other hand, the total gap is never nearly as wide as it could be if all the members of the extreme groups exhibited extreme characteristics. (For score (a) the gap between man./prof. and unskilled represents 22 per cent of the maximum possible range; (b) 28 per cent, (c) 30 per cent, (d) about 30 per cent, and (e) 47 per cent.) In addition, there is little consistency over exactly where on the continuum the other groups are to be found.

All this goes to show that social tendencies based on an analysis of groups cannot be read as 'laws' applying to individuals, as one might have expected from reading some accounts or from taking too literally some of the arguments in other parts of this chapter. This is

Table 41 Some measures of differences between groups*

	Man./ prof.	Other non-manual	Skilled manual	Semi-skilled	Un-skilled
(a) Average number of deprivations (from p. 178)	0.47	0.95	1.33	1.78	2.22
(b) Average percentage giving a typically lower-class response to questions on child-rearing	39	44	56	59	67
(c) Average social class of sons (man/prof=+2 unskilled=−2)	+1.0	+0.7	+0.3	0	−0.2
(d) Average age of sons' finishing education (years)	17.1	16.7	15.6	15.4	15.3
(e) Average level of quali-fications (no quals=0, higher ed=2)	0.97	0.70	0.35	0.15	0.07

* The detailed derivation of these scores is described in note 22

well illustrated by trying to deduce a 'law' as to why people become unskilled manual workers. It is known that unskilled workers experience all sorts of difficulties, and that certain types of people tend to become unskilled workers. But it is not possible to find any group of people for whom unskilled status is inevitable. Only 9 per cent of those without any educational qualifications,[23a] only 12 per cent of the sons of unskilled fathers,[23b] only 10 per cent of the chronically ill middle-aged,[23c] and only 10 per cent of all coloured immigrants or 20 per cent of Pakistanis,[23d] are unskilled workers. These figures, which refer to men alone, are high only in relation to the fact that only 5 or 6 per cent of all men are unskilled. They *are* high, and an inspection of the wider statistics on job opportunities will show that they are part of a very serious tendency for certain types of people to have restricted opportunities, but they will not bear the weight of any theories of social predestination.

Much more still needs to be known, therefore, about exactly what sorts of people are prone to deprivation, and about the details of the interactions between the different aspects of deprivation. Analysis based on groups of people, to which this book has necessarily been limited, gives a strong indication of what to look for, but an analysis of individual people will be necessary before any true understanding of the social process can be reached. Nevertheless, in spite of the imprecise definition of groups, it seems that membership of particular groups is an important factor in determining deprivation risk, and those groups are the ones that have been described as 'socially weak'.

It is not clear to what extent such groups are weak because they are composed of individuals who are themselves weak, or, on the other hand, whether the members are weak because they belong to the group that is weak as a result of external social forces. No doubt it is both, and the relative importance of external and internal weakness no doubt varies with the particular group under consideration. Nor is there any reason why the relation should not be changed. Elderly people may tend to be weak as individuals; the present pension arrangements are an external factor that reduces their weakness as a group, but not enough.

It is vitally important to an understanding of deprivation, and to the formulation of future policy, that the distinction between the individual and the group, between internal and external weakness, should be recognised, and the role of each considered. For years academic and political debate about poverty and deprivation has been polarised between those who look only at the individual and those who look only at the group. The social-psychological approach is to ask why this individual is weak, and how, or even whether, he can be made stronger. The sociological approach is to ask why this group is weak and how it can be made stronger. To parody the opposing approaches in a manner of which the proponents themselves are sometimes guilty, the emphasis on personal factors is seen to imply personal inadequacy as the source of deprivation, while the emphasis on structural factors is seen to imply an imposition of deprivation on the minority by a selfish society. While both these extreme viewpoints would seem to suggest that deprivation is here to stay forever, a more careful consideration of the internal and external sources of social weakness may well suggest that something can be done. If the debate degenerates into an argument as to whether the poor are 'deserving' or 'undeserving', we shall get nowhere. It is obvious that some are poor through misfortune and others through mismanagement; both deserve help if help can be offered. The question is: how? And there is by now sufficient evidence to show that the answer to that question should not be tied too closely to a stereotype of the individuals in a group, based on the average of that group. For instance, in Chapter 4 it was shown that, while, on average, children of unskilled workers are less likely to be good readers than the children from higher status homes, the variation within the group is still substantial – almost as great as the variation among all children.[24]

In seeking to understand deprivation, then, it is going to be necessary to consider both the personal characteristics of those who experience it, or who are at risk, and also their circumstances – both the social skills and/or vices of the people, and the structure of the society in which they live. In seeking to formulate policy, perhaps, the emphasis will be more on structural and circumstantial factors, because these are more likely to be influenced by government intervention; nevertheless, personal characteristics must be considered, to help decide which policies are most likely to be effective.

Let us start with personal characteristics, considering first the 'social vices' that have been associated with deprivation, and then the lack of social skills that is sometimes suggested as the source of the problem. There are various forms of deviance, often clearly anti-social, which are known to be much more common in deprived areas, and among deprived people, than in the more prosperous sections of society. It is even possible to identify specific cases where specific forms of deviance – perhaps alcoholism or mental illness – have led an individual directly into poverty, and therefore into apparent membership of the deprived class. This has led to the assumption that depravity and deprivation are one and the same thing, and even that the first is the direct cause of the second. Yet the word 'deprivation' implies literally that something has been taken away from the sufferer – something which, by implication, he is entitled to. It is a socio-economic characteristic, observed by comparing one man's situation with that of his fellows. Even if it is true (which it has not yet been demonstrated to be) that there is an exact relation between them, there is no logical inevitability that such socio-economic characteristics (deprivations) are one and the same with behavioural characteristics (depravities). Yet it is almost impossible to mention the word 'deprivation' in conversation without personal faults being introduced into the discussion. On the other hand, the association between the two in the public view has led many of those who sympathise with the poor to reject all considerations of social psychology. The baby has gone with the bath water.

The fact that various forms of deviance are to be found in places and classes similar to those suffering from economic deprivation cannot be used to explain the incidence of the latter. In the first place, although the two phenomena are found in similar sorts of places and classes and not much among more prosperous groups, this does not mean that they follow exactly parallel courses. As has been found in

Monmouthshire (see p. 157), they are distinguishable geographically; and even where they are to be found in the same area or class, that does not imply a relation between them within the people of that area or class. Secondly, even if deviance led to deprivation, no one would suggest that all the deprived are deviants. Thirdly, if a causal relation exists, it is possible to suggest that it is the deprivation that leads to deviance; that when the material conditions assumed by the wider society do not exist, social behaviour cannot be expected to conform. It has been shown both among societies and in experiments with animals that, for instance, severe overcrowding tends to generate abnormal, self-destructive, mutually destructive or isolationist behaviour.[25] Finally, there are many cases in which it is not the deviance itself that causes this deprivation but the attitudes and behaviour of the rest of society; for instance, bringing up children without a father.

There is, indeed, one way in which a deviant social characteristic can be seen to lead to more acute deprivation. All groups contain some people who manage well and others who manage badly. Among the deprived this difference in the ability of the householders to keep their home uncluttered, to budget within the weekly income, to keep clothes in repair and so on, can make all the difference between a low but tolerable level of living and abject squalor. For people in a given situation, all other things being equal, it is certainly the case that incompetent housekeeping would effectively intensify the problems of deprivation. But it is equally certainly not the case that such incompetence can lead us to distinguish between the 'deserving' and the 'undeserving' poor: that the problems of deprivation are the problems of 'non-copers'; or that non-coping is responsible for deprivation. There are copers and non-copers in all ranks of society; but for the most part the distinction is unrecognisable because there is nothing to be coped with. Deprivation is necessary before coping with it can start. It is tempting to connect the two by identifying non-copers as the deprived, or the deprived as non-copers. Not so long ago a famous study of children categorised mothers as good or bad managers merely by looking at the state of the children's clothing, without considering the financial circumstances. We can now see that both aspects need to be considered. Deprivation is not a result of not coping; on the other hand, that should not stop us trying to help people to cope, until the deeper problem of deprivation is solved. Nor should rejection of non-coping as a cause of deprivation lead us to reject all aspects of social psychology from our study of the incidence of misfortune.

Specific 'social vices', then, do not much help towards an explanation of deprivation nor towards the formulation of policy. In so far as they cause deprivation, there is not much that can be done about it; insofar as they are caused by deprivation, an end to the deprivation should put an end to the 'vices'. But another aspect of personal characteristics deserves more careful consideration: the social and cultural characteristics that place the socially weak at a disadvantage in a competitive society. It is necessary to understand these characteristics, which undoubtedly exist, not in order to saddle the deprived with the responsibility for their own misfortunes, but in order to work out how to alter external circumstances to prevent those misfortunes.

Under the heading of 'social skills' there are three separate but interrelated factors: 'intelligence', as measured by I.Q. tests; 'culture', as indicated by attitudes to child-rearing, education, and work; and education. All these exhibit differences between those occupationally defined social groups which, as we have seen, exhibit different levels of deprivation. On the other hand, as with deprivation, there is variation within each of the social groups. For instance, the semi-skilled and unskilled groups account for far more than their fair share of 'mild mental retardation' (defined as about I.Q. 50-75), whether the subject's social group is determined by his own or by his father's occupational status. But these mildly retarded individuals constitute only the lower tail of a wide distribution of I.Q. within those groups: with any normally distributed characteristic, the group with the lowest average score is bound to have a disproportionate number of individuals in the lower tail of the general distribution. Moreover, unlike the members of most other I.Q. strata, the mildly retarded continue to improve both their I.Q. and their social adjustment throughout youth and into early middle age.[26] ('Severe mental retardation' (I.Q. below 50) appears to be a purely biological phenomenon, and exhibits none of the traits of mild retardation mentioned here.)

There is no space here for a proper discussion of the enormous and contentious subject of the sociology and psychology of social classes. As a basis for the discussion of possible policy, however, two suggestions can be made. First, to a large extent the social psychological characteristics of lower-status groups are not *inferior* to those of the higher-status groups on absolute criteria; they are *different* from characteristics that have come to be associated with success. Secondly, these different social-psychological characteristics are largely determined by differences in socio-economic circumstances. At the very least the social-psychological characteristics would be altered if the socio-economic circumstances were altered.

There is research evidence in support of both these contentions, although there is also research evidence in support of contradictory hypotheses.[27] If we can assume that they are partly true, then policy based upon them would be partly successful, which would at least be better than a do-nothing policy based on the assumption that those of low status are innately less capable than those above them in the social hierarchy. If the hypotheses suggested above are correct, the chain of cause and effect goes something like this: below average socio-economic circumstances induce different social-psychological characteristics; these characteristics are not those with which success is associated, and which education is geared to measure and promote; as a result, those who exhibit these characteristics are unlikely to achieve educational and occupational success, and are therefore able to aspire only to low-status employment, and below-average socio-economic circumstances, and the vicious circle starts another turn. This hypothesis suggests two optimistic conclusions. First, if socio-economic deprivations that do not depend directly on this education-occupation cycle – in housing, in health, in social security provisions – could be eliminated, then the circumstantial inequality that plays so important a role in the cycle would be eroded. Secondly, if the power of social institutions to discriminate between individuals with varying social-psychological characteristics could be identified and reduced, this ought to lead to greater equality and less risk of deprivation. According to our hypothesis, social-psychological characteristics do not cause inequality to exist but are the medium for its perpetuation. They certainly influence the rank in the social hierarchy in which any individual can expect to find himself.

This last sentence is important, because it may provide the key to the conflict between arguments based on individuals and arguments based on groups. It is quite clear that any individual member of a group will do better than other members of that group if, for instance, he does well at school. That appears to hold true for society as a whole if we compare the earnings of *men* with varying levels of qualifications, or if we compare the earnings of *women* with varying

Table 42 Median earnings of full-time workers with varying levels of educational qualification, 1973[28]

	No qualifi-cations	C.S.E. etc.	O level etc.	A level etc.	Higher educ'n	Degree etc.
Men	£1,630	£1,770	£1,800	£1,890	£2,420	£3,000+
Women	£ 840	£ 990	£1,250		£1,560	

levels of qualifications (Table 42).

But what may be true of the individual male or the individual female, compared with others of their own sex, does not hold true between men as a group and women as a group. When the members of the two groups are placed in competition with each other, it becomes clear that sex is at least as important as education in determining income levels. It may be that a similar distinction exists between social classes, in the link between education and well rewarded employment; it almost certainly exists between classes in access to education itself.

Since government policy can directly influence social institutions, but can hope to influence personal characteristics only indirectly through that medium, it is necessary to consider the role that institutions play in the relation between social-psychological characteristics and socio-economic circumstances that has been postulated. Perhaps the key question is whether the greatest happiness for the greatest number is best pursued by institutions that try to make each individual as 'happy' as he possibly can be, or by institutions that try to bring all people up to a common level. Since education is known to play a role in the relative distribution of prosperity, and since it has long been the institution to which hopes of greater equality have been pinned, let us consider that question for education, before looking at policy and institutions in other fields.

At some time not so very long ago half the adult population could read, write and perform simple arithmetical tasks. A smaller proportion had reached an educational level rather beyond these elements. No doubt those who could read were more prosperous than those who could not, and less prosperous than those with better education. It was clear that, for the individual, learning the three Rs would considerably reduce his deprivation risk. So, one might have argued, universal elementary education ought to have eliminated deprivation. Unfortunately, while the less educated half of the population were (most of them) learning to read and write, the better educated half were moving on to O-level standard and the best educated minority were getting degrees. Relatively, deprivation risk remained the same. Thus, it was not inability to read and write itself that left the lower orders in an unequal position, but their educational position relative to others. Similarly, while getting O-levels is now a good way out of deprivation for the individual (according to Table 42), it will not be a means to eliminate deprivation itself if those who now have O-levels go on to get A-levels. Yet, since the essence of the qualification by examination is to distinguish between people who can and cannot pass the examinations, the essence of education for qualifications must be to retain inequality of achievement, even if that were based on equality of opportunity. Education will promote greater equality if the tendency is towards more and more people having *exactly* O-levels, but not if the tendency is towards more and more people having *at least* O-levels.

As with education, other social institutions have naturally developed to promote the welfare of those who are within reach of them, leaving those out of reach at a disadvantage. For the most part there is neither purpose nor truth in any suggestion that such institutions were developed by a selfish elite anxious to promote their own advantage; on the contrary, many developments can be seen as an effort to reduce the gap between the elite and the strata immediately below them – qualification by examination being a principal example. Institutions pursuing the prosperity of the individual through the 'top-down' strategy have naturally arisen in a society where the individual's prosperity is important. Nevertheless, there comes a point at which the effect of the continuation of that strategy is to increase the isolation of those beyond its reach; at that point it becomes necessary to adopt the 'bottom-up' strategy to prevent deprivation.

These points are well illustrated in a field that has not been discussed elsewhere in this review of deprivation – personal mobility. It will be no surprise that households without a car are much more common among the lower-status groups than among the higher (Table 43).

Table 43 **Percentage of households without a car, by socio-economic group of head of household, 1972**[29]

Professional/managerial etc.	15
Other non-manual	48
Skilled manual	45
Semi-skilled	69
Unskilled	82

The distribution of car-ownership between social groups is not unexpected, and can be explained largely in terms of the distribution of income (not entirely, because many cars are bought by companies and used by their senior or intermediate non-manual employees out of working hours as well as on firm's business). But, until the past few years, almost the whole of government transport policy was geared to making it easier and easier for people to get about by private transport. Not only was public policy aiding and abetting private advantage in this way, but also it became progressively more difficult to get about by public transport and on foot. Public transport atrophied (especially in rural areas) as demand for it dried up; and it was slowed down by congestion in towns – precisely the areas where private cars are least necessary. Even now many planning decisions favour car-owners. Public facilities such as shops are being concentrated into larger units but further apart, not in order to suit the car-owner but nevertheless having that effect. This is to say nothing of the non-transport costs of a private transport policy, in pollution, noise, accidents, limitations to pedestrian movement, energy consumption and so on, which affect all of us. Yet the nearest we have come to a general restriction on private mileage is through taxing petrol, a policy which in any case will mainly affect those only just able to afford a car. On the other hand, there is some evidence that even car-owners would accept collective restrictions on car usage in situations where individual abstention would be useless, in return for both environmental benefits and reduced congestion.[30] And the more the private transport strategy is pursued, the more need there is for people to buy cars, while those without become even more restricted.

The same example also illustrates how the gap between deprivation and privilege is a function not only of economic status but also of social status more widely defined; for the benefits of the motor car are biased not only towards those with higher incomes but also towards adult males, who dominate all fields of social activity. Children, old people and women are largely left out. While two-thirds of all men are licence-holders, only one-quarter of women are.[31] A recent PEP survey in the Outer Metropolitan Area has shown that the majority of mothers in car-owning households are without transport during the week, as their husband takes the car. More than half the mothers *even in car-owning households* do not hold a licence,[32] so that in transport, as in housing, employment and many other fields, most women are dependent on their husbands. If they have no husband, they are stuck.

But the main lessons to be learnt from the transport example suggest new lines for policy. First, pursuit of the individual's welfare can lead not only to relative inequality for those unable to profit from it; even an absolute lowering to the level of service for the disadvantaged (in public transport); and even, in extreme cases, a level of service worse for those who do profit from it than would exist if the individual advantage had never been pursued in the first place (through congestion). Secondly, given such an individual policy, it is virtually impossible for the individual who appreciates these problems to help the situation by opting out of his advantage. Thus, if some individuals forego the use of their cars in congested cities, the temporary improvement in traffic flow will immediately be counteracted by other people who are encouraged to use their cars after all. The individual with a conscience signs over his advantage to someone else, without helping the disadvantaged at all. Similarly, in education, the individual who sacrifices his chance to go to university allows someone else to take his place, suffering a considerable loss himself to no purpose. Only a collectively decided policy can achieve his objective.

It is not, of course, suggested that the day after the motor-car was invented the government should have decided either to ban it, or to provide one for every home. There came a point, however, when the continued encouragement of mobility for certain individuals began to imply disadvantage for others; and more recently a second point at which the nature of the problem came to be appreciated. That was the point at which the bottom-up collective policy should have replaced the top-down individual policy.

How then do policies and institutions in the other fields considered in this book appear in the light of our distinction between benefits for individuals and benefits for all. Education, while apparently intended for all, nevertheless favours the individual. Social security provisions are clearly in the 'all' category, but are hamstrung by their administrative inefficiency, and by our insistence that they should leave a large part of the field clear for the individualist strategy of private insurances and pensions. Municipal housing is an undoubtedly collectivist policy; its failure to achieve all its objectives may be ascribed partly to the continued individualist institution of owner-occupation, if also partly to the imbalances in the location of people, jobs and homes. The Health Service is another case of a universalist intention achieving more for some individuals than for others; the search for the cause and for the solution must be based not only on physiological and sociological research, but also on market research, bearing in mind the possiblity that change in the product and its salesmen may be required to increase consumption. Employment policy seems too diffuse to be summarised in these terms; there is often conflict between industrial and economic goals, on the one hand, and social goals on the other. Paradoxically, the traditional concentration of the manpower service on manual workers in general, and the unemployed in particular, is a short-term bottom-up policy that may hinder bottom-up progress in the longer term. If the job market service could be more successfully provided for the whole range of occupational strata,[33] there might be more scope for influencing mobility between strata.

About the public services most closely associated with the concept of deprivation and multiple deprivation – the personal social services – hardly a word has appeared so far in this book. This has been partly because the personal social services do not fall under the heading of any of the particular aspects of deprivation that are the subject of each of the earlier chapters, and partly because it was necessary to discuss the relation between the individual and the group before the role of these services could be clearly understood.

The personal social services combine two roles, perhaps rather uneasily. One is to assist those who exhibit the personal characteristics associated with personal failure and social maladjustment to cope with their problems, and, if possible, to make use of what opportunities there might be to escape from the worst misfortunes of deprivation. It has been argued earlier in this chapter that such personal characteristics are not basically the root source of deprivation; on the other hand, those individuals who exhibit them are highly likely to be deprived, and until a more general social solution to deprivation is found, there is no reason why these most unfortunate people should not be given a helping hand. The offer of a helping hand, however, should not be seen as an alternative to a fundamental solution, in which case the social services would be doing more harm than good.

The other role of the personal social services is that of providing an agency through which those in need are linked with the various services intended to help those in misfortune. There are many such services – one might almost say too many different ones. Social workers should be in a position to maximise delivery to the target group, but at present they are ill-equipped to do so, in training, in personnel, in powers, by red tape, and so on. One family may be deprived in several different ways, eligible for assistance from several different sources, and under the wing of several different social workers.

If one of the conclusions of this book is that unfair inequality requires some pretty basic restructuring of educational and occupational opportunity, another is that some of its worst excesses could be mitigated if all the various policies aimed at deprivation could be put together and made to achieve their intentions. Perhaps such administrative improvements could be put in hand while consideration is given to whether and how the more general structure of inequality can be tackled. A start has been made on improving delivery, through the attack on multiply-deprived areas for instance, but the lessons learned need to be given wider application. Research is needed into the administrative complications that lead to the failure of co-ordination, and into the consequences of such failure for the client groups. Market research is needed to find out why client groups are failing to buy the services on offer, and a marketing policy should be adopted to sell them. Above all, information is needed about individuals, to find out who is multiply-deprived, who is at risk, and how multiple deprivation works. For lack of detailed information at the individual level all the evidence and all the theories about multiple deprivation are necessarily based on the collation of information about groups of people.

The theme of this book has been that the present extent of deprivation is based on the present structure of inequality. That does not mean, however, that only complete equality can eliminate deprivation. It should be possible for policy to aim at a level of inequality, without which no complex society has been known to exist, which avoids those unnecessary and unfair misfortunes that have been called deprivation. Nor does a long-term policy on inequality avoid the need for other policies that provide direct and immediate assistance for those who are now in trouble, and cannot wait for a long-term policy to take effect. Both these sets of policies will require a political will for collective action, which must be based on the realisation that deprivation is a misfortune, not a sin.

NOTES

1 R. Lawson and B. Reed, *Social Security in the European Community*, Chatham House/PEP European Series, No. 23, 1975.
2 O.P.C.S., *General Household Survey 1973*, H.M.S.O., 1976
3 A. I. Harris, *Handicapped and Impaired in Great Britain*, H.M.S.O., 1971.
4 O.P.C.S., *G.H.S. 1973, op. cit*. The estimate of 'about another three million' is derived from the fact that the rate per thousand reporting a limiting long-standing illness, *including* a handicap of impairment, is just under double the rate per thousand given by Harris for handicap or impairment *alone*, of which there are over three million (see note 3).
5 For detailed qualitative and quantitative descriptions of the problems of disability, see respectively S. Sainsbury, *Registered as Disabled*, Bell, 1970; and A. I. Harris, *op. cit*.
6 C.S.O., *Social Trends 1975*, H.M.S.O.
7 *Ibid*. The Social Commentary at the beginning of the 1975 issue of *Social Trends* has collected together a wide range of statistics showing differences between Social Classes.
8 *Ibid*.
9 a) O.P.C.S., *G.H.S. 1973, op. cit*.
b) A. I. Harris, *op. cit*.
c) Central Statistical Office, *Social Trends No. 5*, H.M.S.O., 1974.
d) O.P.C.S., *G.H.S. 1973, op. cit*.
e) 1971 *Census*.
f) *Ibid*.
g) *Ibid*.
10 R. Lawson and B. Reed, *op. cit.*, quoting figures from T. Wilson (ed.), *Pensions, Inflations and Growth*, Heinemann, 1974. But see also M. Young (ed.) *Poverty Report 1975*, Maurice Temple Smith, 1975, for a detailed comparison between Britain and Germany.
11 (a) O.P.C.S., *G.H.S. 1973, op. cit*. The figure gives the proportion of households with fewer bedrooms than deemed necessary by the O.P.C.S. 'bedroom standard'.
(b) O.P.C.S., *G.H.S. 1973*, H.M.S.O., 1973. The figure gives the proportion of households that do *not* have the exclusive use of both a bath/shower and a W.C.

(c) I.L.E.A., *Literary Survey 1971.* The figure gives the proportion of 11-year-old children whose reading test score was in the lowest 25 per cent of the combined distribution. See Chapter 4, p. 124.

(d) O.P.C.S., *G.H.S. 1973, op. cit.* The figure gives the proportion of men aged 45-64 who report limiting long-standing illness.

(e) 1971 *Census*: see p. 128 of Chapter 5.

(f) Dept. of Employment, *New Earnings Survey 1975.* The figure gives an estimate of the proportion of male workers whose gross earnings were less than £45. See Chapter 5, p. 132, and especially note 6(2).

(g) *Ibid.* The figure gives the proportion of male workers who worked over 48 hours in a particular week.

(h) Unpublished data from the survey reported in W. W. Daniel, *The PEP Survey on Inflation,* PEP Broadsheet No. 553, 1975. See Chapter 1, p. 46.

12 These chances are calculated by assuming that each misfortune is an independent risk – not at all a good assumption, but used for the sake of illustration. Thus, for a member of the top group, the chance of *escaping* all eight misfortunes is $0.97 \times 0.95 \times 0.93 \times 0.89 \times 0.98 \times 0.93 \times 0.95 \times 0.93 = 0.61$. The chance of *not* escaping all of them is therefore 0.39.

13 i.e. $0.07 \times 0.11 \times 0.07 = 0.0005$;
$0.38 \times 0.33 \times 0.45 = 0.056$.

14 A. Hunt, J. Fox and M. Morgan, *Families and Their Needs, with Particular Reference to One-Parent Families,* H.M.S.O., 1973; Department of Health and Social Security, *Report of the Committee on One-Parent Families* (the Finer Report), H.M.S.O., 1974.

15 David J. Smith, *The Facts of Racial Disadvantage,* PEP Broadsheet No. 560, 1976.

16 A. Little and C. Mabey, 'Reading Attainment and Social and Ethnic Mix of London Primary Schools', in D. Donnison and D. Eversley (eds.), *London: Urban Patterns, Problems and Policies,* Heinemann/C.E.S., 1973.

17 David J. Smith, *op. cit.*

18 Letter to *The Times,* 22 October 1974.

19 L. Syson and M. Young, 'Poverty in Bethnal Green', in M. Young (ed.), *Poverty Report 1974,* Maurice Temple Smith, 1974.

20 Based on Table 1 on p. 15. Note that these figures refer to 'collapsed socio-economic groups' not to 'social class'. The main difference is that 'intermediate non-manual workers' (about 5 per

cent of the total) appear in the 'professional/managerial' social
class, but in the 'other non-manual' socio-economic groups.

21 See, for instance, J. Askham, 'Delineation of the Lowest Social
Class', in *Journal of Biosocial Science,* vol. 1, no. 4, October
1969.

22. These scores are derived as follows:

(a) From the summary of deprivations on p. 178 of this chapter; the
percentages have been summed across all eight deprivations and
divided by 100.

(b) From the Central Advisory Council for Education (England),
Children and their Primary Schools (the Plowden Report),
H.M.S.O., 1967, vol. 2, 'Research and Surveys'. Taken from
Appendix 3, 'The 1964 National Survey', Tables 16, 17, 19
(Q52b), 21 (Q.12), 21 (Q.20), 21 (Q.33), 23, 26 (Q.30d), 27, 28
(Q.43b), 32, 44, 49, 53 (item 5, attended as percentage of
provided), 61, 65, 66. All these tables contain an analysis by social
class which exhibit a strong tendency for the upper classes to give
one kind of response, and the lower classes to give another kind
of response, to a question indicating the parents' attitudes or
behaviour towards schooling. The score is derived by adding
together the number of times the typically lower-class response
was given, and dividing by seventeen, the number of items in the
analysis. Only questions concerned with attitudes or behaviour
not likely to be dictated by the parents' material circumstances
were included. In general, the responses tend to show a greater
interest in the child's school progress among the upper classes.

A similar analysis of attitudes and behaviour on child care
produces very similar results (using data from J. & E. Newson,
Infant Care in an Urban Community and *Four Years Old in an
Urban Community,* Allen & Unwin, 1963 and 1968).

(c) From O.P.C.S., *G.H.S. 1971, op. cit.,* based on hitherto unpublished data kindly made available by O.P.C.S. For fathers in each
occupational group the average occupational status of their sons
is calculated by means of the following scoring system:

Managerial/professional	$= +2$
Other non-manual	$= +1$
Skilled manual	$= 0$
Semi-skilled manual	$= -1$
Unskilled manual	$= -2$

(d) *Ibid.* For fathers in each occupational group the average age at which their sons left school is calculated on the following assumption:

Under 16.0	=15.0
16.0-17.11	=17.0
18.0-19.11	=19.0
19.0 or over	=21.0

(e) O.P.C.S., *G.H.S. 1973, op. cit.* Table 4.7. Whereas the previous score is based on the education of the sons of the members of each occupational group, this one is based on the education of the members of each group themselves. The scoring was as following:

No qualifications at all	=0
Qualifications normally obtained at school	=1
Higher education quali-fications	=2

23 (a) O.P.C.S., *G.H.S. 1973, op. cit.*; (b) O.P.C.S., *G.H.S. 1971, op. cit.,* based on hitherto unpublished data; (c) O.P.C.S., *G.H.S. 1973, op. cit.*; (d) David J. Smith, *op. cit.*

24. See Chapter 4, p. 124 and note 24. The coefficient of variation among children in the unskilled group is 16.6, and among the whole range of children 16.8.

25. See, for instance, J. B. Calhoun, 'Population Density and Social Pathology', in *Scientific American,* 1962; and 'The Role of Space in Animal Sociology', in *The Journal of Social Issues,* 22(4).

26 See M. Rutter and N. Madge, *Cycles of Disadvantage: A review of research,* Heinemann, forthcoming; and Ann M. Clarke and A. D. B. Clarke, *Mental Deficiency, the Changing Outlook,* 3rd edition, Methuen, 1973.

27 See Rutter and Madge, *op. cit.,* and C. Jencks *et al, Inequality.* Allen Lane, 1974.

28 O.P.C.S., *G.H.S. 1973, op. cit.* The figures have been standardised for age. The full title of each of the categories (in the opposite order to that given in the text) is as follows:

Degree or equivalent
Below degree higher education
G.C.E. 'A' level or equivalent

        G.C.E. 'O' level or equivalent/C.S.E. grade 1
        C.S.E. other grades/commercial/apprenticeship
        No qualifications.

29 O.P.C.S., *G.H.S., 1972.*
30 See the Independent Commission on Transport, *Changing Directions,* Coronet Books, 1974; and M. Hillman, I. Henderson and A. Whalley, *Personal Mobility and Transport Policy,* PEP Broadsheet No. 542, 1973.
31 *Changing Directions, op. cit.*
32 M. Hillman, I. Henderson and A. Whalley, *Transport Realities and Planning Policy,* PEP, forthcoming.
33 As, for instance, in Sweden. See Santosh Mukherjee, *Making Labour Markets Work,* PEP Broadsheet No. 532, 1972.